# The
# Marine Aquarium
# Manual

*To my mother for all her help and encouragement*

# The Marine Aquarium Manual

**Maurice Melzak**
Illustrations by Sheila Galbraith

ARCO PUBLISHING, INC.
New York

Published by Arco Publishing, Inc.
215 Park Avenue South, New York, NY 10003

© Maurice Melzak 1984

Library of Congress Catalog Card Number: 83-73166
ISBN 0-668-06124-3


Printed in Great Britain

# Contents

# Acknowledgements

The author would like to thank Richard Sankey and Richard Christmas for their help in the preparation of this book.

Also sheila Galbraith for the illustrations and Dick Ogilvie for the back jacket photography. Front jacket photography by the author.

# Introduction

This book is for those fascinated by the sea, marine life or the sea shore who would welcome an opportunity to keep marine organisms in the home. Marine aquaria were once believed to be extremely complicated but today there is no mystique surrounding them and anyone interested can set one up. Those keeping tropical fish in freshwater aquaria already have some experience as well as most of the equipment needed to transfer to marines, though it will be important to change the material of the filter bed. But even those with no experience of aquaria can buy cheaply the aquarium, pump and other essential components and follow the simple instructions to set up the marine system. Because they are not complicated and do not require constant maintenance, they can be set up by young people, or at schools and colleges, so unusual and unfamiliar living creatures can be observed and studied. These include anemones, looking more like flowers than animals, hermit crabs living in discarded snail shells, whelks, prawns, starfish and limpets. All of these animals can be kept plus many more including various species of unusual fish. Together they will provide a constant source of interest and the chance of observing behaviour never seen before by anyone else, for there is still much to be learnt about marine life.

This book particularly stresses the importance of setting up an aquarium based on the 'natural system' – an aquarium that reflects as closely as possible a true picture of the marine world. There will be many rocks gathered from the sea, covered in seaweeds, a host of fascinating invertebrates and maybe one or two fish. So the aquarium will try to display a true picture of marine life, with its inhabitants living in some sort of harmony resulting in a more stable aquarium system. Too many marine aquarists take advantage of highly efficient modern filters enabling them to fill their tanks with large numbers of fish while ignoring the other components of

7

the marine world, the rocks, seaweeds and invertebrates. Their aquaria seem sterile environments relying totally on artificial filtration. Though filtration is important in more natural systems, it is essentially backing up a natural cycle, and this will be explained more fully.

This book is all for people keeping organisms they can gather themselves from the shore, though it may be justifiable to keep foreign species for educational or research purposes for example. In temperate countries such as Britain, or parts of New Zealand, North America or South Africa the sea is usually cooler than room temperature. The marine aquarium will therefore use cold water, though it is not vital to chill the water artificially because many seashore inhabitants are quite able to live at room temperature, provided it is not too warm. Some people may live by warmer waters, the Mediterranean or even tropical seas, so their aquaria may need heating. Both cold water and warm water systems are dealt with in this book.

There are many reasons, to do with ecology and conservation, why it is preferable to keep organisms that are personally gathered. Commercial exploitation is avoided, for one, and species that are rare or which will not live long in the aquarium can be left. The seashore, the region where the sea meets the land, is populated by marine organisms specially adapted to cope with tidal conditions and the resulting alternating exposure to sea and air. A visit to the shore, particularly a rocky shore, is a rewarding experience with beautiful scenery combined with an incredible diversity of organisms. Many of these species are introduced here and it is hoped this book will help to increase people's respect for, knowledge and awareness of one of nature's most fascinating environments.

# 1 Major Components

## AQUARIA

Aquaria today are made entirely from plate glass held together by a silicone rubber sealant. It is often a surprise to people that the aquarium needs no reinforcement at all when full of water.

A good size to start out with for the first marine aquarium is 2 ft by 1 ft by 15 ins high. This '2 foot' tank will contain about 13 imperial gallons of water and though this may sound a lot it is really the minimum to maintain a healthy and stable community of creatures. From this point of view a '3 foot' is even better but to begin the '2 foot' tank is less costly, takes up less space, and due to its smaller volume and fewer inhabitants will be easier to maintain.

The tank can be bought from your local aquarist's shop which will probably sell all the equipment described in this book.

If you buy the aquarium, it will be a neat job and guaranteed not to leak, though one can buy ¼-inch-thick plate glass and construct the aquarium oneself using aquarium sealant. But before this is done some points are worth considering. First, it may not be much of a saving, if at all, for aquarium manufacturers can buy glass at very low prices, often as double-glazing off-cuts. Second, not only will the home-made aquarium probably not be such a neat job as the professionally made one, but it may also leak, so will then have to be emptied and resealed at the point of the leak. Finally, working with glass is dangerous and great care must be taken not to cut oneself.

In this book there will be references to a '2 foot tank' or even '3' or '4 foot' tanks. These are standard measures for aquaria, and in all cases the height is about 15 ins and the width one foot. There are conversion tables at the back to help those more familiar with metric units and though metric units are used later on in the book, in describing aquaria feet and inches are still more familiar units.

Before the aquarium is put in position remember that a 2-foot tank will contain about 130 lbs weight of seawater, and a 3-foot tank about 200 lbs. This will mean a strong stable base will be required.

For aquaria that will not need to be heated, it is important to site them away from radiators or sunny windows; preferably in a cool room.

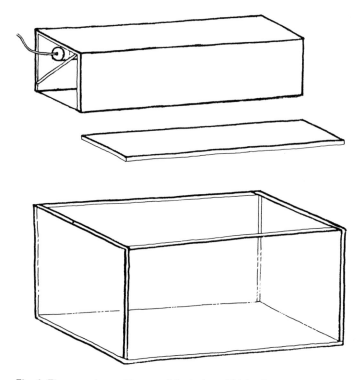

**Fig. 1** The aquarium with a possible design of lid that has a compartment for the lighting and a separate section easily removed for feeding.

## THE LID

It is important for a marine aquarium to have a lid, not only to reduce the evaporation of water and prevent dust and dirt entering, but also to house the fluorescent light which is the most widely accepted way of illuminating the tank. Lids can be bought and must be made of glass or plastic; metal will rust. A glass lid can also be made at home using aquarium sealant.

One possibility is to have an easily removable strip of glass 2 ft by 6 ins (for a 2-foot tank) covering the front half of the tank. The back portion is designed to house a fluorescent light and can be put together with aquarium sealant and covered with a white adhesive plastic often used to cover shelves. This will hide the fluorescent tube and help to reflect the light downwards.

## THE WATER

The marine aquarium will require saltwater and many people regard this as a major hurdle in the setting up of an aquarium. But this problem is very easily solved. Either you can gather water from the sea, or, if this is impracticable use artificial seawater, which is a perfectly acceptable alternative.

Seawater is a living dynamic fluid containing a variety of different constituents. These include various inorganic substances, such as minute concentrations of metals and salts, a host of living organisms ranging in size from bacteria to whales, and organic substances that are produced by all the plants and animals in the sea. Planktonic life is also an important constituent of natural seawater and it includes bacteria, single-celled plants, and a host of animals, some the larval stages of familiar sea creatures and some less well-known but extremely important permanent residents. These include protozoans, crustaceans, medusae and worms.

It is important for the marine aquarist to try to make the constituents of his aquarium water resemble as closely as possible that of the sea, and this can be done with varying degrees of success. It is simple, and important, to ensure there is the right concentration of salts in the water by using a hydrometer. Regularly changing a few pints of the water will replace the essential minerals and trace elements taken out by the aquarium inhabitants. Organic substances will be produced by organisms in

11

**Fig. 2** A selection of microscopic marine plankton. From the top:
the larva of a brittle star;
a *Copepod*, a permanent member of the plankton;
the larval stage of a crab, called a zoea;
a jellyfish or medusa;
a mysid larva;
the larva of a blenny.

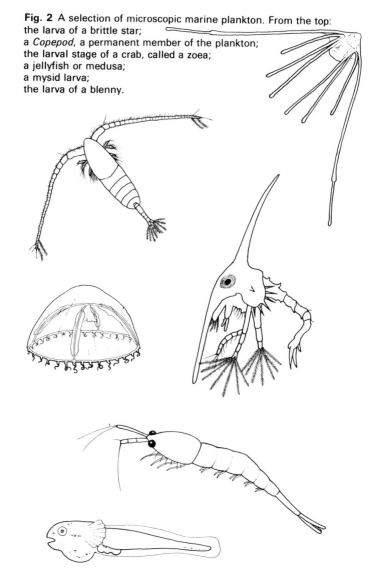

the aquarium and these will be supplemented by the addition of food. The final ingredient of natural seawater, the planktonic life, is far less easy to maintain for long in the aquarium. Many marine aquaria are perfectly healthy and well-established habitats without most of these organisms, though certain forms of planktonic life will exist in the aquarium to the advantage of all the inhabitants. By adding natural seawater to the tank, planktonic life will be introduced, though some aquarists will not put natural seawater in their aquarium. They believe it may add pollution, harmful bacteria or other detrimental factors, a rationale which might apply to large-scale commercial set ups. But for the home aquarium, especially where native marine organisms are kept, clean natural seawater is of great benefit to the aquarium.

So bear in mind the danger of polluted water and find an area where the sea is clean. When water is collected either wade out a few feet to avoid picking up the debris brought in by the waves, or collect the water from a deep rock pool that has recently been filled by the sea or, best of all, use a boat and collect the water a little way out from the shore. Remember to ensure the water is pure seawater too, and not diluted by a nearby river or any other freshwater; estuaries are not good places for gathering seawater. A shore with abundant and diverse flora and fauna strongly suggests the water in that area will be suitable for the aquarium.

For those who do not have ready access to the sea, it is possible to use artificial seawater for the bulk of the aquarium's contents. One can buy proprietary brands of aquarium salt at the aquarist's shop and, using freshwater from the tap, dilute it to make up a quantity of sterile seawater. A new, clean, plastic dustbin is best used for this, or if this is not possible, a plastic dustbin carefully sealed and lined with a strong plastic bin liner. Find out approximately how much water the plastic bin will hold (1 cu ft of volume contains about $6\frac{1}{2}$ imperial gallons). If the bin volume is around 2 cu ft then buy a 10 gallon salt pack, or its equivalent, put it in the bin and then add the 10 gallons of water using a vessel of known capacity, say a 2-pint jug. Once you know where the 10 gallon level is, mark if off with a pencil on the outside of the bin for future reference.

The first large volume of seawater can, of course, be made up

**Fig. 3** In mixing artificial seawater, besides the large plastic bin, these three items are essential. First calculate how much water is needed, then buy the appropriate salt packs. Except for the first mix which can actually be done in the aquarium, put the salt in the bin and fill the bin with the right amount of water. This is where a vessel of known capacity is useful. Once the water is added, and aeration has helped the salt to dissolve, check it is of the right concentration, or specific gravity using the hydrometer.

actually in the aquarium but after that quantities must be made in the plastic bin.

What are the advantages of using artificial seawater? The first is convenience. Bags of the salt can be bought for varying quantities of seawater. It will be explained later that a small quantity of seawater – around a gallon or two – must be regularly changed, so if there is a bin of seawater already mixed, part of it can be used at a time. Making up artificial seawater in clean conditions at home ensures none of the potential hazards of pollution are introduced into the aquarium.

When the aquarium is set up at least a gallon of the water, though, must be natural seawater – not artificial. This is because important micro-organisms will be introduced, crucial to the well-being of the aquarium inhabitants, but even in this case the water can be from an established aquarium, assuming of course it is in good condition and well maintained. There will be more about this later.

For people not having easy access to the sea, carrying large quantities of water back from the coast may be a problem and this is another advantage of having the bulk of the aquarium water made up at home.

For those who live near the sea, and who have good access to unpolluted water, some money will be saved by dispensing with the need to buy the salt packs, but apart from that users of artificial seawater lose very little. It is, though, always worthwhile to consult your local aquarist's shop to ensure it is safe to use local tap water for mixing up artificial seawater. In Britain where chlorine is added to tap water there are no problems, but in some parts of the world certain compounds are added to the water that may harm the aquarium organisms.

## LIGHTING

Light is essential for the marine aquarium and there are three main ways of lighting the tank: incandescent light bulbs, fluorescent tubes and newer types such as the mercury discharge tube.

Two electric light bulbs of say 60 watts in the lid of the tank are adequate to light the tank but are not the ideal solution. This is mainly because of the heat they emit whilst they are on. So if light bulbs are used they should be in the form of spot lights, at least 6 ins above the tank. In this case the lid need only be a flat transparent sheet of glass, not the type that can contain a fluorescent tube.

Fluorescent tubes are generally considered as a better way to light the aquarium than light bulbs. They are cooler, are more efficient in their light output and use less electricity. To set up a fluorescent light a special ballast box is needed. This can be hidden out of the way behind the aquarium so the heat it gives off does not raise the temperature of the water. There are many different types of fluorescent light; some are made especially for the aquarium and are said to give just the right type of wavelength of light required by marine organisms.

But this is one of the many aspects of keeping a marine aquarium which has no hard and fast rule. There are so many different factors that can affect the aquarium that one can never be certain about attributing blame or success to one particular aspect. With regard to lighting a standard cool white fluorescent light might be part of a successful aquarium set-up, whilst a specially made marine fluorescent light might be part of a system that is not doing so well. So if to save money two tungsten spot lights are used there is no reason at all why a successful thriving aquarium cannot be maintained.

All lighting set-ups require a basic knowledge of electricity (see p. 44). Ensure care is taken and the electrical shop where the lights are bought is consulted. They will be glad to help.

Lights in the aquarium should never be on all night. If the room is fairly well lit it will probably be sufficient to have the lights on in the afternoon or just in the evening.

The best system for starting out could well be, for a 2-foot tank, a 2-foot ordinary 'cool' fluorescent tube.

There is a new generation of aquarium lights coming on to the market. One of these is a mercury discharge tube that, though initially expensive, is very cheap to run. These lights last a long time, give light of a suitable wavelength for the aquarium inhabitants, and do not give off much heat. Consult your local dealer who will, hopefully, be up to date on these new aquarium innovations.

All aquaria, especially those with warm water, will contain organisms requiring light at fairly regular periods. Tropical species, for example, are used to about 10 hours of sunlight a day. It

16

is important for the lights in the tank to be switched on and off at a regular time and it may be a good idea to have the lights connected to a time switch so they are automatically turned on and off if the tank cannot be attended daily.

All plants and animals that are continually submerged, especially in the tropics, will be used to more intense periods of illumination around midday when the sun is high in the heavens. At other times much of the sun's radiation will be reflected away by the water surface. So for tropical aquaria especially, if they are artificially lit for about 12 hours a day, then try an extra spot light for a time, after around 6 hours of illumination.

## FILTRATION

In aquarium terminology filtration is a broad term encompassing the various ways the seawater is maintained and some form of filtration is necessary in the relatively small marine aquaria discussed in this book. As will become apparent there are three types of filtration: biological, mechanical and chemical.

In the sea a natural cycle exists, both single-celled and multi-celled plants grow utilizing light and certain nutrients and minerals that are dissolved in the water. The plants may be consumed by herbivores and these plant-eating animals will have their predators, the carnivores. The waste products of marine animals, usually chemicals such as urea, uric acid or ammonia, plus the tissues of all living organisms after death will be broken down by aerobic bacteria; bacteria which require oxygen. After they have broken down the organic compounds substances are released which may again be used in plant growth.

It is possible to set up an aquarium in which this natural cycle takes place. The aquarium would need large numbers of rocks gathered from the sea on which vast quantities of animals and plants are living. With proper lighting, an air stone bubbling away to help in water circulation and a maximum of only one or two small fish, such an aquarium could well support a natural marine cycle and would be called in aquarium terminology a natural system.

But though this sort of system is the ideal, for it is a genuine marine microcosm, its main drawback is that it must normally be of considerable size, with a surface area of at least a few square

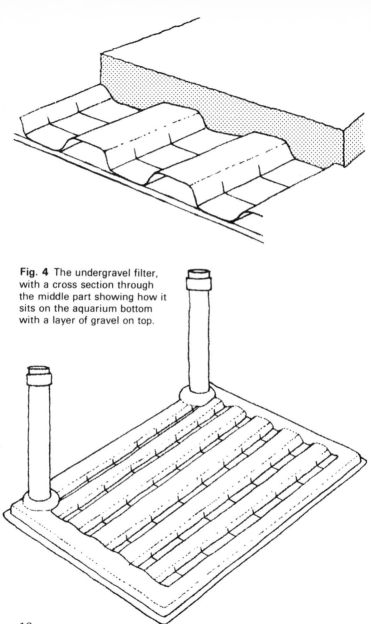

**Fig. 4** The undergravel filter, with a cross section through the middle part showing how it sits on the aquarium bottom with a layer of gravel on top.

metres, to reach any sort of stable balance. Though it must be said there are aquarists who maintain natural systems with much smaller aquaria. Home aquaria should be set up based on the natural system but there are two potential problems to overcome due to their limited size. The first is that there may not be enough room for sufficient rocks that supply a substrate for the beneficial bacteria to colonize. So the waste products produced by the aquarium inhabitants may not be able to be dealt with by the bacteria, thus polluting the water. There must also be an efficient circulation of water around the tank, and this is the second important point.

To deal with these two potential problems in the home aquarium a system has been devised called the undergravel filter. It is essentially a corrugated plastic sheet that fits over the entire floor of the aquarium. It is perforated with many tiny slits and there are also one or two plastic tubes about 2 cm or 1 in in diameter, that rise up from the filter. These tubes are called the uprights or uplifts and are important in ensuring the circulation of water.

On top of the undergravel filter is placed a layer of gravel between 5 and 10 cm (2–3 inches) deep. This gravel will need to be of 2–3 mm grain size; any smaller and it would fall through the perforations. It must also be porous and of a calcareous material, meaning it is formed of calcium carbonate, but this is explained more fully later (p. 23–4). It is in this gravel bed, with its large surface area, that vast numbers of the beneficial bacteria will live and as water circulates it is constantly being drawn through the filter bed where all the waste products of the aquarium inhabitants are broken down. This circulation is brought about by air from an air pump directed, using plastic tubing, down the vertical uplift. In the tube a mixture of water and air bubbles is formed that is lighter than the water alone. So it rises up and out of the tube to be replaced by water that has been drawn through the filter bed and the perforations in the filter. So a constant circulation of water takes place with the water being oxygenated at the surface. Then with dissolved waste products it is drawn through the filter bed and back out of the uplifts into the tank again.

It will be explained later (p. 34–8) that there are more sophisticated methods of filtration but the undergravel filter is a

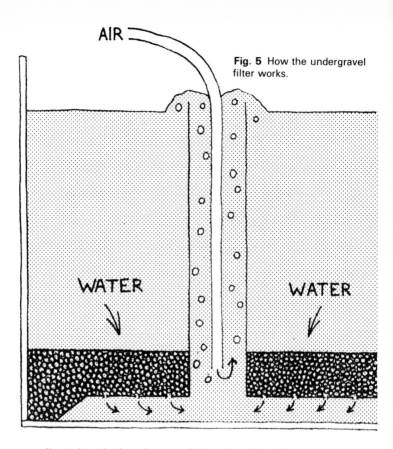

AIR

**Fig. 5** How the undergravel filter works.

WATER

WATER

well-tried method used successfully and preferred by many marine aquarists. There are also variations on the theme, that are also dealt with, such as using an electric water pump sitting on top of the upright instead of using an air pump, or using a power filter in the very efficient reverse flow system.

The undergravel filter acts as a biological filter as it employs the naturally occurring beneficial bacteria, but it also acts as a mechanical filter – in the aquarium there may be suspended particles that cloud the water, but as it is drawn through the filter bed these particles are trapped and so the water is kept clear. Gradually the end product of the bacterial breakdown will collect as a yellowish dusty substance in the filter bed. This is called detritus and though harmless, and in fact beneficial in small amounts as it provides even more substrate for bacteria to colonize, in large amounts it can be easily stirred up to cloud the water or even clog the filter. So about every 12–18 months, assuming the aquarium is not overcrowded, the gravel will need to be cleaned; a process which is explained more fully later (p. 160–1).

So though a natural system is the ideal, representing a genuine marine microcosm, it is difficult to set up in a small home aquarium. The undergravel filter is therefore employed to give stability to the system so if there is a sudden change, the death of an animal for example, it will not upset the balance of the aquarium, but will be efficiently dealt with by the bacteria. Any decomposing matter however should be removed as soon as possible. When the aquarium is set up put in plenty of rocks with seaweeds growing on them, and also a selection of invertebrates but only a few small fish. Try to bear in mind that the natural system, with a sensible balance of inhabitants, would need no filtration, and so consider the undergravel filter as a necessary but underemployed back-up system.

As the undergravel filter, or the other filtration systems mentioned later, are so efficient in harnessing the bacteria to break down potentially harmful substances in the aquarium, some aquarists use them to greatly increase the amount of animals they keep in their aquarium. Often the result is a tank full of fish in a totally unbalanced and unnatural environment. Here the concept of the marine aquarium as a minute section of the sea is totally abandoned in a barren, sterile display. In these aquaria, as no consideration is given to creating any sort of natural cycle, the filtration system often operates close to the limits of its efficiency. So an extra strain on the system – the introduction of yet another fish or the unfortunate but inevitable death – pushes the system over the top. The bacteria will not be able to cope and toxins may build up to a fatal level in the tank. Another possibility is that there will be such a demand for oxygen by the overactive bacteria, as well as the fish, that they will start to die, thus causing an avalanche effect as more poisonous substances build up eventually killing everything in the tank. This extremely distressing 'biological breakdown' is virtually unknown in marine aquaria based on the natural system where there is a balance of organisms living in uncrowded conditions. For the filtration system is always in reserve, and never operates close to its limit of efficiency.

Of course there are cases where the filtration capacity of a marine system needs to be maximized – for example in commercial or scientific institutions where large numbers of organisms, especially fish, must be kept. Often highly sophisticated filtration systems draw water out of the tanks, filter it mechanically, biologically and chemically (using charcoal, ozone or airstripping for example). The water may also be sterilized using ultraviolet light before being re-introduced to the aquaria. These systems are not within the scope of this book, for the purpose here is the setting up of an aquarium that gives a genuine reflection of the underwater world. With a balance of fascinating and unusual animals and hopefully some seaweeds an appreciation of the beauty of these different organisms will be conveyed and a clearer understanding of marine life and ecology gained.

## The gravel
The whole of the floor of the aquarium will be covered with a layer of gravel between 5 and 10 cm (2–3 ins) deep. This gravel should not be small pebbles but rather grains of a calcareous material such as the crushed shells of cockles, or other shell fish (oyster shells may at first cloud the water). Fossil coral commonly known as coral sand is particularly good. The grains must be about 2–5 mm, for if they are less than 2 mm they will clog the filter.

Coral sand can be bought from the aquarium shop. It is formed from coral that was once part of a living coral reef but which died thousands of years ago, become fossilized and has then been broken up by the sea into small grains. It is imported from tropical areas so it may be an expense, though a worthwhile one.

If the coral sand is bought try to find a variety that is high in algal oolites. These are small calcareous discs of fossilized algae, the dominant marine plant. Some algae growing in the tropics use calcium carbonate in their structure. When these plants die and become fossilized they may be broken up by the waves to form small discs. The reason why these are useful is in the fact that besides being calcareous they are very porous, meaning they have a high internal surface area for the beneficial bacteria to colonize.

One can find suitable gravel for the aquarium at the seashore, that complies to a large extent with the criteria of being calcareous, porous and of the correct grain size. There are shores where one can find broken shells or if the shell pieces seem too large they can be broken up a bit more using a heavy stone. These shells must be thoroughly rinsed before being used in the aquarium. This is best done by putting a few handfuls in a plastic bucket: pour on some tap water, swill it around and then pour the water away. Repeat this process a few times until the gravel is clean. Gravel from polluted beaches should not be used and under no circumstances must detergent be used in any cleaning processes associated with the aquarium. Detergent is extremely toxic·to marine life, and after a recent bad oil spill it was shown that the detergent used to clean up did more harm to the shore life than the oil that covered them.

Crushed cockle shells are sold at some aquarist's shops so can be bought and if coral sand proves too expensive then a cockle shell/coral sand mixture will do. Coral sand must be rinsed before use in the way described above for the crushed shells.

## pH and buffers

This is the final section on filtration: there has been an emphasis on the need for the gravel to be of a calcareous nature – i.e. formed from a type of calcium carbonate. It has already been explained that the individual grain size and also the surface area of the gravel is important in the process of biological filtration. The calcareous nature of gravel will help regulate another vital function of the aquarium, the extent to which the water remains at the correct pH. pH is an expression that indicates whether a solution is acidic or alkaline. A pH value of 7 is that of freshwater which is neither acid nor alkaline, but neutral. Acids are of a pH under 7, a weak acid is pH 6 and the stronger the acid the lower the pH. The alkalinity increases with pH values above 7. Seawater has a pH of 8.3 – which means it is slightly alkaline. It is important that in the aquarium the pH remain at this level or at least between 8.1 and 8.4.

The large amount of calcareous gravel acts as part of the buffering capability of the tank, meaning it contributes to resisting alterations in pH in the aquarium though it may quite naturally change slightly in the course of 24 hours due to the metabolism of the plants and animals. Changing some of the water every month or so also helps in pH balance, but more about this in the chapter on maintenance (pp. 150–66).

But what sort of things alters the pH? It seems that the animals and the plants while carrying out their essential life functions, will produce or utilize compounds that may affect this balance.

Respiration and photosynthesis are the most important of these. All living organisms respire in a process that liberates energy for growth and development by breaking down complex organic compounds. Animals obtain these compounds directly or indirectly from plants, but plants manufacture them in a process called photosynthesis. In this process energy is harnessed from light and using carbon dioxide and water as raw materials complex organic compounds, usually carbohydrates, are produced with oxygen being given off as a by-product. In respiration oxygen is utilized and carbon dioxide given off which is exactly the opposite of what happens in photosynthesis. So these two processes can complement each other in the aquarium during the day because though the animals only respire, in the plants the photosynthetic activity greatly exceeds their respiration. At night, due to the lack of light, photosynthesis will not occur but the plants and the animals will still respire. Carbon dioxide levels may build up and it will be dissolved in the water to form carbonic acid, thus lowering the pH.

This fact, combined with the lower oxygen levels of the tank, could produce very hostile conditions but for the fact that the water is constantly being circulated and aerated by the filtration system. This effectively maintains stable conditions by day and by night so no problem will occur.

Plants are important in the aquarium, whether larger fronds of 'macro-algae' or the thin green film of 'micro-algae' which will grow on the glass and rocks in the tank. In a marine aquarium that is established and correctly maintained the pH balance will quite naturally fluctuate slightly, but never reach harmful levels. This is only likely to happen in a neglected or overstocked aquarium, or when the water is not circulated for many hours.

# 2 Additional Equipment

By now the essential processes of the marine aquarium have been explained and the major equipment described. There are a few extra things that are needed, however.

## THE AIR PUMP
There are many brands of vibrator air pumps and your local aquarium dealer will advise you as to a reliable one. For the 2-foot tank air will have to be directed down the two uplifts of the undergravel filter, and so a fairly small pump is needed. If a 3-foot tank is set up it may well be that rather than an undergravel made up of one piece of plastic, two separate UG filters will be needed. In this case there will be four uplifts and so a slightly more powerful pump will be needed, but there are companies that make 3-foot undergravel filters that have two uprights. If a 4-foot tank is set up then two 2-foot undergravel filters will almost certainly be needed.

Some of the very cheap air pumps can be rather noisy, and this can be a nuisance if the aquarium is in a living room. So try to find a quiet model if this is likely to be a problem. Larger pumps are often more efficient and quieter, but also more expensive.

One way of reducing noise from a vibrator pump is to place it on a piece of foam or other soft material. This will also prevent the pump 'walking' off the table or shelf. It is also an idea to keep the pump above the water level of the aquarium thus avoiding, in the rare occurrence of a power cut, the unlikely chance of water flowing back along the air tubing and flooding the pump.

## AIR TUBING
For a 2-foot tank at least 6 ft of transparent plastic air tubing

**Fig. 6**

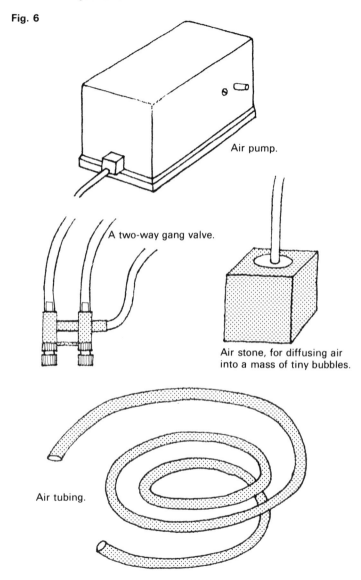

Air pump.

A two-way gang valve.

Air stone, for diffusing air into a mass of tiny bubbles.

Air tubing.

will be needed, depending of course on how far the pump is from the tank.

Extra uses of air tubing include aerating newly collected or manufactured seawater and also in the syphoning of water in and out of the tank.

## AIR STONES
Made either from a porous stone or wood these fit on the end of air tubing and diffuse the air to a mass of tiny bubbles. These are of some benefit but by no means essential.

## GANG VALVES
A gang valve connects the air tubes that are directed down each of the undergravel filter uprights, with the single air tube from the air pump.

Some types are adjustable, which is very useful, because they can control the air flow down each separate upright, for it is only necessary to have a steady trickle of air bubbles coming up each uplift, not a huge gush. A cost-saving alternative to gang valves is to employ a simple T-junction.

## THERMOMETER
It is worthwhile knowing the temperature of your tank. But as the section on cooling explains (pp. 38 – 41), it is not easy lowering the temperature of a home aquarium.

## HYDROMETER
For making sure artificially made-up seawater, or water in the aquarium, is of the right concentration.

## ALGAE SCRAPER
A specially made plastic-ended gadget that will scrape algae off the front glass panel. Plastic ensures the glass is not scratched.

## GLASS OR WOOD ROD
This instrument, that must have a blunt not pointed end, is used in directing fragments of food to each and every animal in the tank.

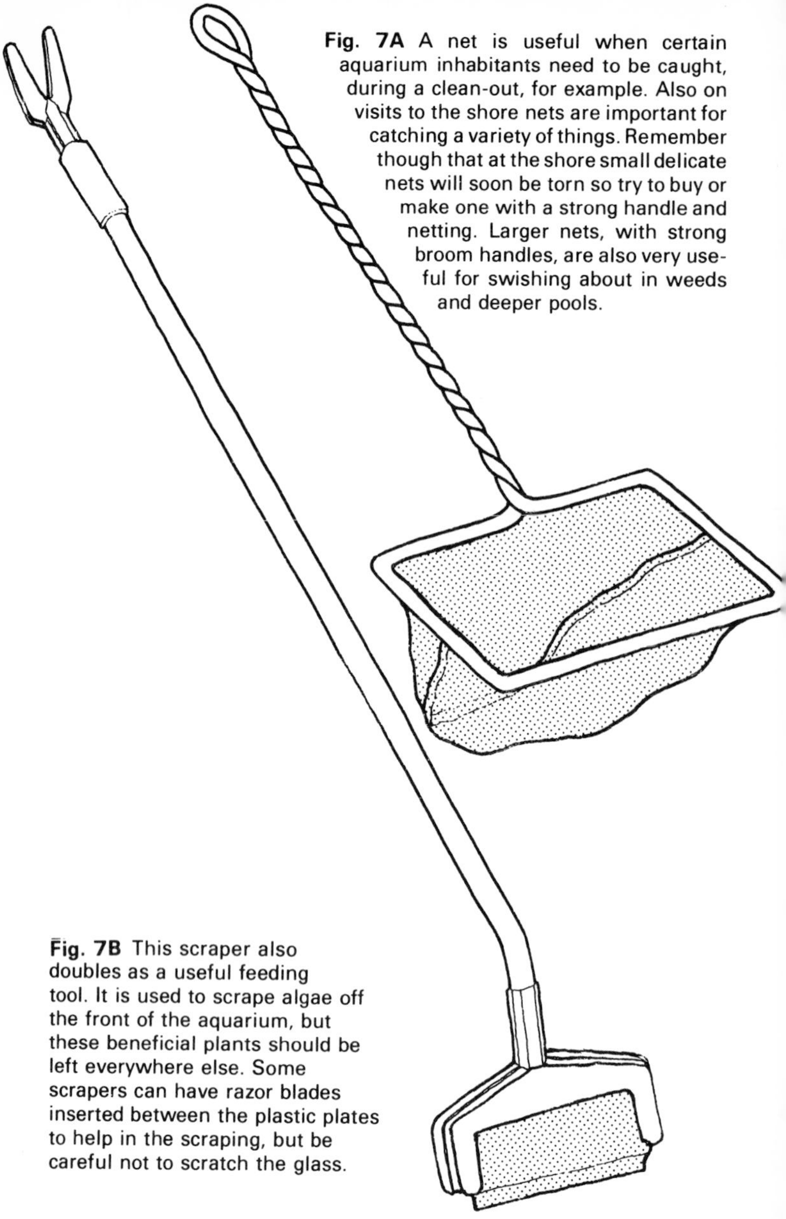

**Fig. 7A** A net is useful when certain aquarium inhabitants need to be caught, during a clean-out, for example. Also on visits to the shore nets are important for catching a variety of things. Remember though that at the shore small delicate nets will soon be torn so try to buy or make one with a strong handle and netting. Larger nets, with strong broom handles, are also very useful for swishing about in weeds and deeper pools.

**Fig. 7B** This scraper also doubles as a useful feeding tool. It is used to scrape algae off the front of the aquarium, but these beneficial plants should be left everywhere else. Some scrapers can have razor blades inserted between the plastic plates to help in the scraping, but be careful not to scratch the glass.

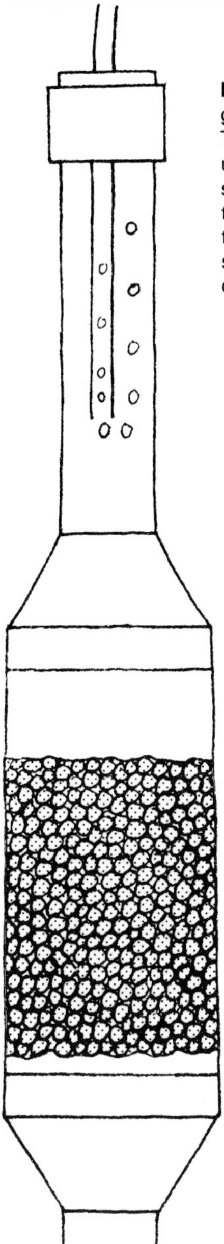

**Fig. 8** The adaptor that can transform an under-gravel filter upright to a charcoal-containing filter. The bottom of the unit fits into the base of the undergravel filter, with charcoal in the middle section, between two layers of filter wood. Air tubing is introduced into the section at the top of this unit and by operating in the same way as the standard upright, water is drawn through the charcoal.

## NETS

For catching and transferring mobile aquarium animals.

## CHARCOAL FILTERS

The use of charcoal does seem to be beneficial to the aquarium, although not essential. A charcoal-containing filter can be bought which works by acting as a substitute for an air lift of the undergravel filter, or charcoal can be placed in the cannister of the power filters mentioned later (pp. 34–8). The first of these works by using the same principle as the air lifts. Water is drawn up the tube and passes over the charcoal in the middle section.

The advantage of using charcoal lies in the fact that the aquarium is a 'closed' system, meaning that the water remains in the tank all the time where it is maintained by filtration. In an open system water would be continually pumped out of the aquarium and new water introduced.

Certain substances given off by the animals and the plants may not actually be broken down by the bacteria in biological filtration, nor trapped by the process of mechanical filtration. Not only may some be toxic if allowed to build up, but they will gradually give the water a yellowish hue. Periodically changing some of the water (which is explained more fully in chapter 7) will go a long way to prevent the build up of these substances, but by using charcoal they are continually being removed from the water.

Charcoal removes these compounds by acting as a chemical filter, for it is extremely porous and so has a huge surface area onto which the particles of dissolved organic matter will adhere or be adsorbed. So as the water is passed through the charcoal some of the harmful substances are adsorbed onto its large surface area, and thus removed from the water.

But there are certain things which must be remembered when using charcoal filters. One is that, although the charcoal has a huge surface area, it will eventually be completely used up and at this point not only will it stop removing some of the harmful substances, but it may suddenly release back into the water part of what has already been taken out. This is called desorption. The best way to prevent this is to regularly change the charcoal in the filter – every two or three months is about right.

It is also possible that certain beneficial trace elements, such as tiny quantities of certain metals, may be removed from the water by charcoal, which can adversely affect the organisms, particularly plants. For this reason some aquarists recommend that charcoal is only used periodically, but with regular water changes which will replace essential trace elements, the constant presence of a charcoal filter is perfectly acceptable.

As the charcoal used in aquarium filtration may be made up of very small granules it is usually necessary to pack it between two layers of 'filter wool'. This is an inert subtance that will hold the charcoal in place and allow a free flow of water through it.

**Fig. 9** The protein skimmer or air stripper. An airstone produces a mass of tiny bubbles that rise up the central tube. It is thought that certain proteinaceous substances dissolved in the water become attached to the bubbles and as they burst at the surface these substances are deposited as a foamy scum in the container at the top. This scum can then be removed.

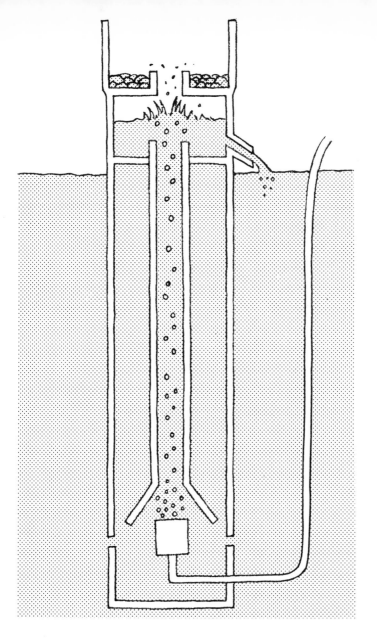

## FOAM FRACTIONATION

Another system exists, probably not as effective as the charcoal filters but worthy of mention, for some experienced marine aquarists do consider it useful.

It involves a technique called foam fractionation whereby aquarium water is vigorously mixed with air bubbles in a special tube. The result is a foamy scum which is chiefly formed from the dissolved organic substances.

It seems that, whereas in the charcoal filter the dissolved substances become attached to the charcoal, in this system they are attached to the air bubbles and are then deposited as a tiny skin when the bubble bursts, thus gradually forming a scum on the surface of the water.

The diagram on p. 31 of a typical system using foam fractionation commonly called a 'protein skimmer' or 'airstripping device', explains how it works.

It would be impossible to say if the two systems, charcoal filtration and foam fractionation, remove exactly the same compounds, or which is better. But the charcoal system is cheaper, less complicated and is probably more effective. So it seems the better choice.

## ELECTRIC PUMPS FOR THE UNDERGRAVEL FILTER UPRIGHTS

It was described how the air pump, by producing currents of bubbles, causes water to flow out of the undergravel filter uprights. It is possible to substitute the air pump/air tube system with an electric pump that sits on top of one of the uprights.

The advantage of this is that it is much more powerful than the air pump system in the amount of water it sends out of the upright. The water in the aquarium will be circulated, and so filtered, at a faster rate.

It is no great loss to have no air bubbling up, for most of the gas exchange in the tank occurs at the surface anyway, and if there is some degree of water movement at the surface, this is enough.

Another small advantage is the fact that water movement through the gravel filter bed is virtually the same at all parts, whether near or far from the upright. So for a 2-foot tank, for example, with a 2-foot undergravel filter only one upright need be included in the system. This is because the powerful electric pump will move enough of the water via the one upright.

Is this preferable to the standard air pump system? Possibly. But it is not vital by any means, and if the charcoal-filled adaptor recommended earlier is used the system might not fit together. So ask your dealer about this first.

# 3 Alternative Filtration Systems

## EXTERNAL CANISTER OR POWER FILTERS

These are filters that are situated outside the aquarium. They consist of a powerful pump that can draw water out of the tank and then force it back again, after it has passed through the filter medium in the cylindrical canister. The filter medium may be a foam-rubberlike substance, useful in mechanical filtration or charcoal for chemical filtration. Other filter media are also available.

Though a filter like this may be used to simply draw water out of an aquarium and return it after filtration, to good purpose, there is one way of using this type of filter in conjunction with the undergravel filter that many marine aquarists find extremely effective – the reverse flow.

The principle involves water being drawn through the filter bed in the reverse direction to normal by means of water being sucked out of the tank and then re-introduced by being directed down an upright. Before entering the tank proper, the water must rise through the filter bed. Besides the benefit of an extra filter for the tank, when the filter bed needs cleaning, which will be very rarely, it is a simple task to swap over the connections of the tubes to the pump for a few hours. So water will be sucked down through the filter bed and the detritus, that has tended to collect on the underside, will be drawn out; though in these systems detritus will tend to collect very slowly due to the mechanical filtration in the canister, and this would be a good time to clean or change the filter media. When cleaning the tank in this way one might also just direct some of this dirty water down the sink and replace it with fresh seawater, as part of the regular water change. With this

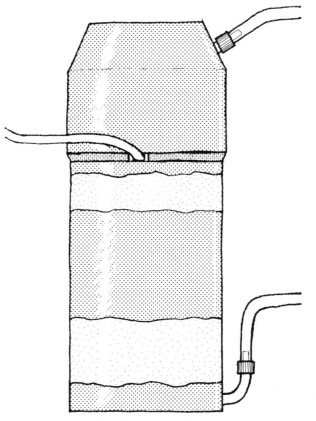

**Fig. 10** A power filter.

system the connection from the canister filter to the undergravel filter upright must be very tight and secure so water will not escape at this junction. Also only one upright per undergravel filter is needed, and where, in a large aquarium possibly two undergravel filters are used, then insert a T-junction so water leaving the pump has its flow split in two for the two uprights.

In this case it is important to ensure the filter's pump is powerful enough to cope with this extra flow. Generally the bigger the filter and pump the better it is for the water will circulate faster. Also if one wants to incorporate a cooling unit in the system the pump will be powerful enough to push the water through that as well. One disadvantage of this system is that certain planktonic organisms may be removed from the aquarium, and with a simple air-driven undergravel filter this is less likely to happen. Though to some extent this is offset by the fact that as water rises up from the filter bed anything in the water will have a tendency to stay there rather than be slowly drawn downwards. It is also possible that when natural seawater is introduced into the tank, the filter is turned off for a few hours, but if this is done do not do it with the aquarium in the dark, only when the aquarium is illuminated by natural or artificial light. Besides the extra efficiency of these systems and the slow build up of detritus one other small advantage is that the tank will be comparatively silent, with no noise from a vibrating air pump or rising bubbles.

## ATMOSPHERE EXPOSED FILTERS
This system was first used in public aquaria in the last century, and is only for the enthusiast with a tank that is 3–4 ft long. These filters are expensive so contact your dealer about cost and advice on setting up.

The principle behind these systems is quite interesting. Basically it is that the bacteria that break down the toxic waste products of the aquarium are kept outside the tank, rather than being in the filter bed. They are actually cultured in tiny granules that offer a large surface area, in a principle similar to that of the coral sand mentioned earlier. Water from the tank is drawn out by an electrical pump. It is then passed through a coarse mechanical filter medium to remove some larger particles, then possibly charcoal but the final stage is the important part, for some of the water is slowly trickled over the granules. These granules are not submerged under water but open to the air which can freely circulate around them. So the essential bacteria always have plenty of oxygen which is crucial to them for the efficient breakdown of the poisonous waste products. On top of that carbon dioxide and possibly other gasses, too, are not passed back into the water but diffuse straight into the atmosphere.

So not only is the bacterial breakdown more efficient, it puts no strain on the oxygen levels of the tank.

On a tank set up with this type of filter no other equipment is necessary. The floor of the aquarium can have a thin layer of coral sand, where some beneficial bacterica will live, but this layer must not be so deep as to become anaeorobic and foul. These systems seem like a good idea, but many aquarists do have problems with them, especially at the beginning. If they are used, the aquarium inhabitants must be introduced into the tank very gradually over a period of weeks, starting off with only one or two organisms. This will give time for the right sort of bacteria to colonize the filter granules, and in adequate numbers to cope with the breakdown of toxic waste products.

## TRAY FILTERS

Some aquarists use the principle of atmosphere exposed filters to construct a filter that works using pumped air and uplifts.

The aquarium is set up with a thin layer of coral sand on the bottom, only a few millimetres deep. A plastic tray is securely and firmly fitted inside the top of the aquarium, but above the surface of the water. The tray needs a rim about 5 cm high, such as the type used in plant propagation. Holes are drilled in the base of the tray and it is filled with a layer of coral sand and sandwiched between two layers of foam rubber. Two uplifts are attached to this box and when the air tubing is inserted water rises from the tank and enters the filter tray. It then sinks through the top layer of foam, where mechanical filtration takes place, then through the gravel where biological filtration occurs, and then through more foam before entering the tank via the holes.

The larger the tray the more coral sand it will hold so its efficiency will increase. So as not to block out the lights it might work with two smaller trays, one at each end, with the lights in the middle.

The system might be tried by the aquarist keen on experimentation. Some have found it an efficient and easily maintained system, for cleaning the filter is no problem. Most aquarists, though, prefer the more conventional systems.

This just serves to illustrate the point that marine aquarium keeping is an area where, though there are simple well-tried methods, there is room for ingenuity, and experimentation. New filtration systems are constantly appearing on the market, but don't be too impressed by gadgets. It is not necessarily true that the more money you spend on equipment the better aquarist you will be or the better your result will be. Much of marine aquarium keeping depends on common sense, experience and the observing and understanding of the organisms. There are countless stories of highly successful aquarium systems using the cheapest and simplest undergravel filters, and aquarists spending a small fortune on the latest filters and having appalling losses. Marine aquarium keeping is a science and an art.

## TEMPERATURE

### Cooling units

The temperature of the sea around a temperate coast, such as Britain for example, varies from about 5°C in winter to 17°C in summer. Room temperature in most people's homes is around 22°C which will mean that the aquarium water will always be above its summer temperature. Some organisms will not be able to live at the high temperatures unless some sort of cooling system is employed. Fortunately the many and varied organisms of the intertidal zone – the area of the shore exposed at low tide – are very hardy and can withstand the higher temperatures. Chapter 5 contains a description of many of these different species.

But what if one wants to keep a cooled aquarium at say an average of 14°C? Well, there are a variety of solutions that generally require a lot of money or a lot of ingenuity. There are special cooling units that can be ordered through more specialized aquarium shops but these are very expensive. It is possible to improvise using refrigerators, and these diagrams illustrate some possibilities.

Most suggested designs involve the use of an old refrigerator that contains a reservoir of seawater in a large glass or plastic vessel. Two pipes connect this reservoir to the aquarium, one for water to enter the vessel and one for water to return back to the aquarium.

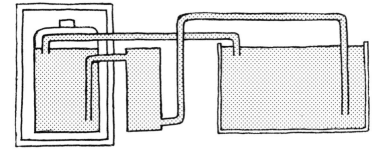

**Fig. 11A** In this cooling unit diagram the power filter draws water out of the aquarium and after filtration passes it into a reservoir, a large plastic vessel, in the fridge. Having such a water reservoir is very useful as it effectively increases the capacity of the aquarium, giving greater stability to the system.

From the reservoir water is returned to the aquarium, possibly by a syphonic or a simple gravity overflow system.

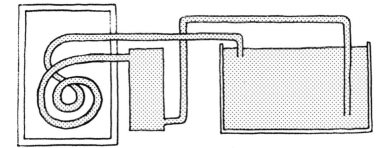

**Fig. 11B** In this diagram, rather than having a water reservoir in the fridge water remains in the plastic tubing thus dispensing with the need for a potentially problematic return system. The tubing travels through the fridge, before going into the tank, and the closer the contact with the ice box the more efficient the cooling will be. It is possible to enclose the ice box in a perspex box and fill this with antifreeze. Then if the tubing is directed so that a few coils are inside this container, then the cooling efficiency should be increased.

Remember whenever cooling is used insulate the back, sides and base of the tank; polystyrene foam is one suitable material for this.

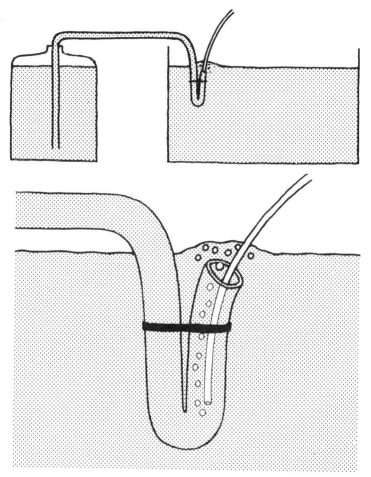

**Fig. 12** This is a possible way of shifting water from a reservoir to the main tank. It involves using plastic tubing of slightly larger diameter than the normal air tubing. When this is bent over (ensure no kinks occur that may cause a blockage), the air tube is inserted as shown. The air bubbles cause water to flow up out of the tube, so a current of water flows from the reservoir to the tank. This system could be used as an alternative to syphoning, or in conjunction with a syphon tube.

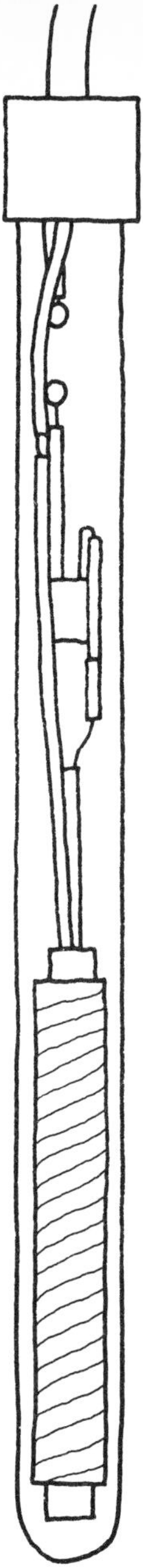

**Fig. 13** This is the combined heater/thermostat unit that is a simple and reliable way of heating the water in warm water aquaria. Remember if the aquarium is ever emptied, in a clean-out for example, always unplug these units, for they will overheat if not continually submerged.

It will be necessary to use a pump of some sort to supply the power to force the water from the tank into the fridge. A siphonic principle can be employed to return the water to the aquarium, though one must always be wary when using this method for if an air blockage for example occurs in the siphon tube, then water will overflow.

·A power filter, a useful tool in any aquarium system, could be used to draw water out of the tank and then force it into the fridge to be returned using the siphonic principle. Or the water leaving the power filter could remain in the tubing, but still enter the fridge. Even if there are many coils of tubing actually in the fridge then cooling will still take place, especially if some are in contact with the ice-box area. This method would not employ a siphon so one potential hazard is removed.

If a cooling system is used insulate the back, sides and base of the aquarium with a material such as polystyrene. Keep an eye on the temperature in the tank; 10-15° C is probably in the right region. If the water is much cooler than this the cooling unit need only be employed for a few hours a day. In winter it may be that no artificial cooling is necessary at all. It will be of no advantage if the water is too cool and a possible result of this may be condensation on the glass of the tank, especially in a humid room.

## Heating

For those fortunate enough to live by warmer seas it may be necessary to heat the water to keep the aquarium water temperature in line with that of the sea. This is no problem at all, for cheap but sophisticated combined heater and thermostat units are available, housed in a long cylindrical tube. Some are particularly easy to adjust so their temperature setting can be altered to fit in with seasonal variations in the sea temperature, or they can simply be switched off if not required for a period.

# 4 Setting Up - Step by Step

After testing that the aquarium does not leak if it is home made place it on a stable, secure base. Remember a 2-foot tank when full of water will weigh over 130 lbs, so ensure the floor boards are not strained and that the object on which the aquarium is placed will be able to support the weight. If a stand that concentrates the weight at the four points of the legs, is used for a tank over 3 feet long, then spread the weight out more evenly by placing the stand on a large plank of wood, rather than risk the unlikely event of breaking a floor board.

It is useful to place the aquarium directly onto a surface that has a slight amount of give in it; polystyrene ceiling tiles are ideal but any thin foam rubber will do. This ensures the base of the aquarium is not strained in any way as it sits on the stand.

Once the aquarium is in position, get the lid and lights sorted out. If fluorescent lights are to be used put the light holder/lid unit in position. Place the 2-foot fluorescent tube inside the lid and make sure it is wired up properly with a switch in the circuit for easy turning on.

Before anything is put in the aquarium ensure that it is clean. This means wiping the glass with a clean damp cloth or sponge – and always ensure no detergents are used for these are highly poisonous. Just use a damp cloth and warm water.

Now the aquarium is clean put the undergravel filter in position on the bottom of the aquarium. For the 2-foot tank one undergravel filter 2 ft ×1 ft will entirely cover the bottom of the tank. If a 3-foot tank is being set up two undergravel filters, each 18 ins ×1 ft with two extra uplifts, will ensure a greater turn over of water, though one unit 3 ft × 1 ft will be adequate.

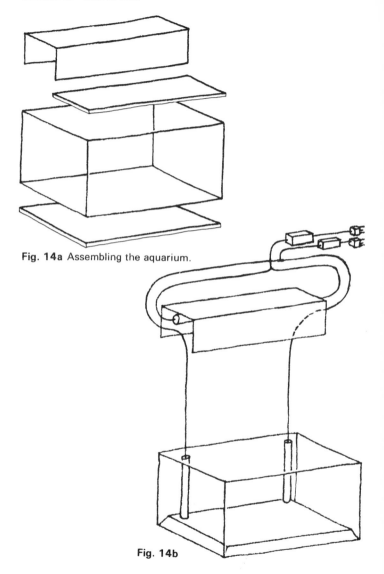

**Fig. 14a** Assembling the aquarium.

**Fig. 14b**

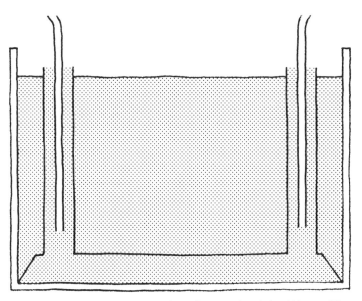

**Fig. 15** The aquarium, showing where the water level should be, and the position of the air tubing in the uprights.

**Fig. 14b** A diagram of the layout of the lighting and air tubes.
The fluorescent tube, which is best housed in the lid that sits on the top of the aquarium, has to be connected to a ballast box. This box which heats up when the light is on, can be placed out of the way. The ballast box is connected to the electric plug, and an on-off switch can be placed in the circuit.
The air pump is connected to a two-way gang valve. From this two air tubes are directed down each of the undergravel filters' uprights. As only a steady, gentle trickle of air bubbles need come from each of the air tubes, it does not really matter where the water level is in relation to the top of the uprights so long as it is within an inch of them.
If the aquarium lid is constructed at home remember to have holes in the side so the air tubing and electric wires can easily enter the tank.

But let us continue assuming a 2-foot tank is being set up with one undergravel filter. It will probably be necessary to fit in the uprights first of all.

Remember that if the charcoal filter attachment is being used it will substitute for one of the air lifts. So when the uprights are in position (with or without the charcoal attachment), place the filter plate on the bottom of the aquarium with the uprights at the back.

Try to ensure that there is a seal between the filter plate and the glass floor of the tank for it is important that no gravel can get under the filter, though in reality a bit always manages to do so with no serious results. If a large amount of gravel gets underneath the filter works less efficiently.

Once the UG filter is in position gently start to add the gravel. What types of gravel, and how it should be cleaned has already been explained (pp. 22–3). Starting from the centre of the filter plate gradually pile in the gravel until a fair weight is firmly holding the filter in place so keeping the seal with the glass. Then gradually smooth the gravel out so the whole of the filter is covered to a depth of 5–10 cm (2–3 ins).

Now is the time to add the seawater. In the 2-foot tank there will be about 13 imperial gallons of water, so unless this quantity is to be gradually collected from the shore a large quantity of artificial seawater must be made up.

Let us start off by assuming only a limited amount of seawater can be obtained and the bulk will have to be made up artificially. It was explained earlier how a clean, plastic bin could be set up, but for the first major 'salt mix' it is easiest to pour enough dry aquarium salt onto the gravel of the 2-foot tank to make exactly 10 gallons of saltwater and then gradually add 10 gallons of freshwater. This will come to about 12 cm or 5 ins from the top. The water must be added carefully. To avoid disturbing the gravel bed try pouring the water into a glass or plastic bowl on the bottom of the aquarium so the gravel is not shifted.

When the 10 gallons of freshwater are added, then start the air pumps and get the water circulating through the undergravel filter. From now on the pump will continually be working. The air tubing can be connected up as shown (p. 44) and if the charcoal filter is to be inserted it can be set up and put in position. It may be that at this point the water level in the aquarium is still too low, so no water comes out of the uprights. If this is the case, to hasten the dissolving of the salt just stick one of the air tubes directly into the water for a few hours.

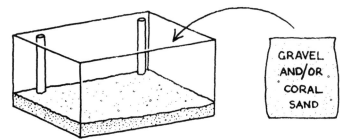

GRAVEL
AND/OR
CORAL
SAND

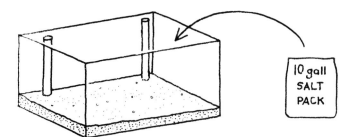

10 gall
SALT
PACK

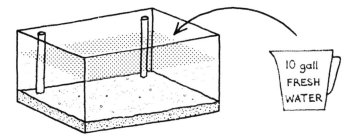

10 gall
FRESH
WATER

**Fig. 16** Adding the gravel and salt water.

It may take an hour or two (according to the brand) for all the salt to dissolve and when it appears to have done so, test with the hydrometer. It is unlikely that the water will be too diluted, unless you have added much more than 10 gallons, but very probable that the hydrometer will show the water as being still too concentrated. So gradually add a bit more water at a time, until the hydrometer reading is right. Some aquarium hydrometers have a mark at the right level. The correct hydrometer reading for the concentration of seawater in the marine aquarium is around 1.024, though this varies slightly with temperature (see the table on p. 169).

If only natural seawater is being used gradually add it to the aquarium until it is nearly full, when the pump can be turned on to keep the water circulating. The water level should now be about 12 cm from the top, and the pump should be on, with air rising from the uprights. For a temperate region tank the lights can be turned on in the evening. For an aquarium keeping tropical organisms more intense light will be required, for longer periods.

It is at this stage that about a gallon or so of real seawater must be added if artificial seawater was used. The purpose of this is to add the vital micro-organisms that will help break down the poisonous waste products of the future inhabitants. Obviously, if the bulk of the water is from the sea this is not necessary. It is quite possible, if natural seawater is not available, to use water from an established mature marine aquarium. This will contain the necessary micro-organisms, but it should not be first choice, as the established aquarium may have a problem of some sort that you will be inheriting, including the possibility of disease.

From now on the aquarium will be a living system: micro-organisms will be multiplying and if the water is looked at closely it may even be possible to see tiny planktonic creatures swimming around. That is why the pump must be continually running and the lights working. This is the time when the beneficial bacteria will start to build up their numbers and acclimatize themselves to the aquarium. They will need something to work on, some sort of organic input so try scattering a few tiny fragments of fish or prawn flesh, for example, around the tank as raw material for them.

Leave the aquarium in this state for about a week and then

48

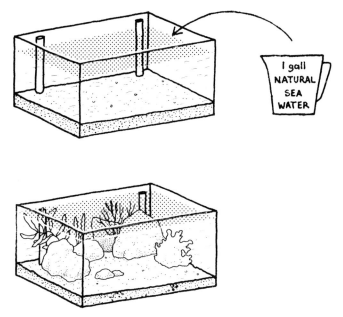

I gall
NATURAL
SEA
WATER

**Fig. 17** Adding the seawater and rocks.

gradually start to introduce the inhabitants. The first thing to put into the aquarium are the rocks, which will not only provide shelter for the larger animals but will also have vast quantities of animals growing on them. It is explained later (pp. 135–9), in the section on collecting, the best way to gather rocks and creatures from the shore.

But it is the rocks that must be introduced into the aquarium first, and as they will have had to have been brought directly back from the seashore, on the same day, it should also have been possible to get some more natural seawater. Add this water first and then the rocks. If the aquarium is full of water by this point then take some out before adding the freshly collected seawater. This will be the first water change (see p. 156).

The level of the water will be gradually getting higher, it should be about 3 cm from the top when the aquarium is finally organized,

**Fig. 18** The cold water aquarium. In the centre is a long-tentacled terebellied worm, a useful detritovore, surrounded by examples of organisms described in Chapter 5.

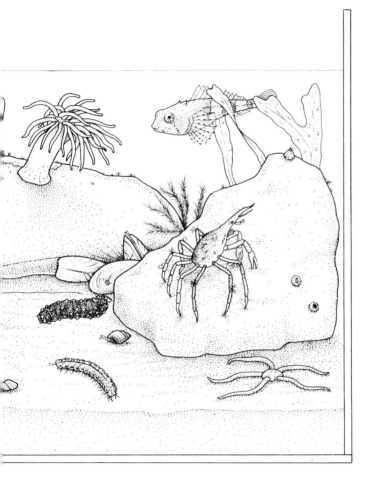

with the top of the uprights level with, just above, or just below the surface.

This stage is one of the most crucial in the life of the aquarium. For it is possible, though highly unlikely, that not enough beneficial bacteria have been developed from the original introduction of natural seawater a week earlier. So when the rocks are introduced, with their attached inhabitants, the danger is that the influx of living organisms might produce wastes that cannot be dealt with by the too-few bacteria. The result will be a build up of poisonous matter in the tank that will kill all the inhabitants. But this is a very unlikely eventuality and would only happen if all the aquarium inhabitants were introduced too soon.

Put the rocks in, and arrange them so a rock is placed in approximately the same position as it was when found, so the creatures on the upper side remain so. It is often a good idea to support larger rocks on a few smaller ones, and to put the larger rocks towards the back of the tank. They can also be piled on top of each other, but it is better not to rest rocks against the uprights, only the back of the tank. Do all the rock arranging carefully – for the tank is made of glass.

Once the rocks are in position, even though during their introduction the water might have been stirred up, the natural circulation continually occurring in the tank will soon clear up the water, and organisms living on the rocks will soon become visible.

Soon after the rocks have been added the anemones, prawns and other aquarium inhabitants can gradually be introduced. The next chapter of the book introduces some of the more suitable organisms obtainable from the seashore.

# 5 The Major Phyla

Once the aquarium has been set up phase two of the operation begins: the actual gathering of the organisms to put in the tank. Though some people will choose to buy them, it is far more exciting to visit the shore to gather the rocks and native marine species personally.

This chapter introduces the phyla or major groups of plants and animals that will be found on all seashores. Of course in different parts of the world the actual species may be very different but all shores will have at least some representatives of most phyla. In the cool temperate regions the rocky shores will prove to be one of the best hunting grounds. Here the firm substratum will enable a host of different plants and animals to gain a foot hold so there will be an immense richness and diversity of species. These shores will often be dominated by a thick lush growth of seaweeds which will provide shelter for many of the animals.

But as one approaches the tropics, shores take on a different appearance. The abundant seaweeds will not be found, instead corals, rare and usually solitary forms in the temperate regions, grow into massive colonies. These coral reefs contain a variety of different organisms that is unequalled anywhere else on earth.

All over the world, too, there are shores formed of a softer substratum – usually sand or mud. Here, due to the lack of solid areas for firm attachment, the shores may not appear to support a great abundance of life, but this is because many of the inhabitants will be burrowers living out of sight. The conditions of a sandy or muddy shore are not so easy to provide in a home aquarium, yet there are species from these shores that will be perfectly happy living in or on the comparatively shallow gravel-like substratum of

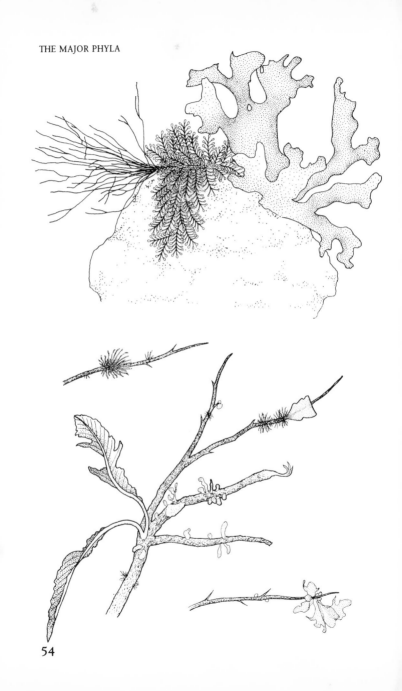

the aquarium. In the temperate regions these include burrowing starfish, sea-cucumbers, crabs and a host of small bivalved molluscs. There are also worms, anemones, whelks and certain fish such as dragonets or sand gobies which will all live in the tank.

## SEAWEEDS

These are the plants of the shore and most are in a group called Algae. Seaweeds occur in their greatest abundance and vigour in the cool temperate regions of the world, particularly on the rocky shores.

Even on the most exposed shores, the vigorous battering of the waves does not prevent at least some species gaining a foothold. Seaweeds provide a host of different sites where the animals of the shore can find shelter and protection, as well as being a food source for many species.

Seaweeds are divided into three main classes according to the colour of their pigments. All plants possess chlorophyll and in the green algae it is the dominant pigment. In the brown algae the chlorophyll is masked by a yellowish brown pigment fucoxanthin and in the red algae the pigment phycoerythrin is dominant. However, colour is not always a reliable criterion in identifying algae; in the brown algae, for example, there are light green, olive green and brown plants. On the shore seaweeds appear limp but, when the tide flows in, the buoyant seaweeds become upright, supported by the water, and sway gently in the currents. If seaweeds were solid and erect, like land plants, the waves would soon break them, so a supple resilience suits their environment.

Seaweeds are usually composed of a holdfast, that firmly attaches the plant to the rocks, a stalk or stipe and a frond. Although the holdfast appears root-like, unlike the roots of land plants it plays no part in the absorption of nutrients but serves only

**Fig. 19** Seaweeds
At the top, from left to right are *Polysiphonia*, *Corallina* and *Porphyra*, all species of red algae.
The seaweeds at the bottom, are *Phycodrys* and a tufted variety of *Polysiphonia* growing on the stem of another algae.

to attach the algae to the rocks. Tug at a large algae and you will see how firmly the holdfast secures the plant.

Algae, in common with all plants, use the sun's energy to turn inorganic substances into organic substances, such as glucose. Animals do not have this ability to manufacture energy rich substances, so must feed on plant or animal matter for their energy sources. In the process called photosynthesis plants trap light and use its energy to convert carbon dioxide and water into carbohydrates. Then in a process called respiration the plants can break down the carbohydrates and utilize the energy for growth and development.

The light of the sun consists of different components – these are sometimes seen separately as a spectrum, in a rainbow for example. Each of the different colours is light of a different wavelength. In the process of photosynthesis pigments present in the plant selectively absorb particular wavelengths of light and reflect away others. The light absorbed supplies the energy for photosynthesis, and in the case of green plants it is the blue and red parts of the visible spectrum. The green part is reflected away and that light is what makes plants appear green to us.

As light travels through water certain colours are absorbed far more readily than others. All red light is absorbed within the first metre, yet blue light, in calm clear water, may penetrate to over 100 metres. (This is why underwater pictures generally have a bluish tinge, for that is the only light available.) As the intertidal algae will be submerged to some extent each day the light essential for their photosynthesis may not be available for some of the time. It could therefore be assumed that as red light can only penetrate centimetres into seawater, the green algae which utilize this light would be restricted to the upper regions of the shore so that when they are submerged it is only in very shallow water. But green algae of varying species may occur at different regions of the shore and this also applies to the reds and browns. This is because the factors that affect where any organism of the intertidal region lives are numerous and diverse. For the algae these may include the occurrence of certain herbivores, resistance to the force of the waves, or the ability to withstand dessication when exposed at low tide. Excessive light can also be a limiting factor and in large doses the ultraviolet light emitted by the sun is harmful to all organisms. It seems that intertidal seaweeds photosynthesize only when under water, so species living in the upper regions of the shore that have brief periods of submergence may be rather stunted species.

The life cycle of seaweeds can be quite complicated. Sexual reproduction occurs when gametes are released and male sperm fertilize a female egg. The gametes may be released from plants producing either male or female gametes, or plants that produce both male and female gametes. These plants are known as gametophytes – the gamete producers.

After fertilization the resulting plant may resemble exactly the gametophyte or be entirely different. The plant resulting from sexual reproduction is called the sporophyte and in these plants asexual reproduction occurs whereby spores are released which grow into gametophytes. In the sea lettuce *Ulva* the sporophyte and gametophyte plants appear identical, but in the kelps or laminarians the large plant of the lower shore is the sporophyte, the gametophyte is a microscopic filament of only a few cells.

Certain brown algae such as *Fucus* or *Bifurcaria* do not have the gametophyte phase, rather the sporophyte produces gametes that fuse to form another sporophyte.

For the seaweeds the intertidal zone provides all the basic ingredients to ensure vigorous growth – water, light and mineral nutrients. There are few land plants that live in such favourable conditions and so it is not surprising that the productivity of the seaweeds, measured by their speed of growth and the bulk of the living plants formed, is greater than in any terrestrial ecosystem, whether tropical rain forest, temperate forest or mangrove. This applies particularly to the kelps of the lower shore and sublittoral zone, for environmental constraints in the upper regions of the shore, such as temperature fluctuations or dessication reduce productivity in these regions. However, a visit to most rocky shores with their thick lush growths of brown algae in particular, will be ample evidence of the favourable conditions for plant growth there.

The production of plants, as seen by their speed of growth or the actual mass of the organism, is an indication of their efficiency in

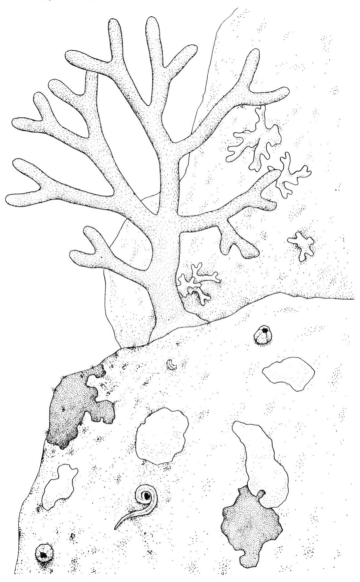

the use of the sun's energy to manufacture organic matter from inorganic substances. This process is known as primary production. Organisms such as herbivores or carnivores obtain their energy from the breakdown of complex organic substances, derived directly or indirectly from plants, a process known as secondary production. The highly productive seaweeds will pass some of the energy they trap from the sun through the ecosystem of the shore, to herbivores and then carnivores and this is one of the reasons why the rocky shore has such a rich diversity of species.

Some of the plants' primary production is used by the plants themselves in respiration and some is directly transferred to herbivores. But even together these two factors only account for a quarter of the total production. Most is actually released by the plant as a leakage of organic matter into the water, where it can be utilized by other plants or animals and some particles of the algae are worn off by wave action. Particles of seaweeds are an important food for filter-feeding animals, especially as the particles are rapidly colonized by nutritious bacteria. Seaweeds also provide shelter for many organisms. Some like fan worms or bryozoans encrust their fronds. Others live protected from rapidly fluctuating environmental conditions under the thick moist mat of seaweeds. Some organisms live in the ramifying holdfasts, particularly of the brown algae, where often a community of worms, crabs, sponges and snails can be found. Finally, there are many species of animals that graze over the rocks such as chitons, sea-urchins or limpets. Young newly settled algal plants often form a large proportion of the diet of these animals.

There are also encrusting algae that are totally different from the more familiar seaweeds. These forms often appear initially as part of the actual rock, though often being quite colourful. These algae incorporate calcium carbonate in their structure and are especially abundant in tropical regions where more conventional algae are less common.

In the aquarium, by adding natural seawater many planktonic forms of algae will be introduced. Often 'micro-algae', single-

**Fig. 20** The green algae *Codium*, showing a rock with encrusting forms of algae, two barnacles and a tube worm.

celled algal forms, will grow all over the glass and rocks to the benefit of the aquarium, though the front panel of glass should be scraped clean for observation. As for the larger species of algae, the 'macro-algae', their spores may be introduced with natural seawater and developed in the tank. Certain species can also be introduced attached to rocks and stones. The greens and reds are particularly suitable, though they are not always easy to keep alive. It may be to do with the light levels, or lack of suitable nutrients or minerals. But certain species will grow; one must just experiment and see.

The brown algae, species such as fucoids or laminarians, must never be introduced into the aquarium. They may emit poisonous chemicals and almost always decay in the tank, so only introduce the green and red algae.

As for the calcareous encrusting forms *Lithothamnion* is a fairly common variety which often occurs in delicate shades of pink or grey, and is likely to be brought back on rocks and stones. Other species like *Corallina* also incorporate calcium carbonate in their structure, and these algae too are worth trying in the aquarium.

## THE ANIMALS OF THE SHORE

Most of the animals likely to be found on the seashore are invertebrates, animals without backbones, and an account is given here of the commoner major groups, or phyla, likely to be found. Some of these phyla contain well-known organisms such as crabs, prawns or starfish but there is an incredible richness and diversity of less well-known species, many of which will be highly suitable for the marine aquarium. Besides occasional visitors to the shore such as sea birds or seals the only vertebrates likely to be encountered are the fish, many species of which can be kept in the aquarium.

The phyla will be arranged, in this book, in a specific order with the simplest animals first and each group following will be of increasing structural and functional complexity. The simplest animals considered will be the sponges, which lack sense organs, with their bodies forming little more than just an aggregation of cells. Higher animals such as the Cnidarians have a more sophisticated body plan with distinct radial symmetry visible. The sense organs are evenly distributed around the outside of a cylindrical or round body. So though there is neither front nor rear, neither left nor right side, the animal is able to gain information on what is happening all around it. Most of the higher animals have developed bilateral symmetry, as seen in worms or fish for example – they can be divided down the middle with each half a mirror image of the other. This body plan is associated with a more active life style, with all the sense organs concentrated in a specific head at the front, or anterior end. So as the animal travels in a certain direction it will be able to use its sense organs to gain information on the environment immediately before it.

Many of the animals that will be found on the shore will be sessile, unable to move throughout their adult lives. These include sponges, bryozoans and barnacles. Others may be described as sedentary, possessing a limited power of locomotion, but generally living within a fairly small territory, limpets and anemones are examples. There are even animals that do have the ability to move about but still remain fairly territorial, such as certain fish. As many inhabitants of the shore do not move around much, if at all, they must be especially adapted in two particular areas. These are feeding and reproduction. Being unable to move means that your food must come to you, and vast numbers of marine invertebrates make use of all the matter suspended in the seawater, as a food source. There is plankton, which consists of single-celled algae, and a multitude of tiny animals, some temporary and some permanent members of the plankton community. There are also particles of organic matter such as fragments of seaweed, and bacteria as well. These animals employ some sort of sieving device that enables them to strain all this matter out of the water, in a feeding strategy described as filter feeding.

The other major problem facing animals with limited locomotory capacity is in the distribution of the species. If adults cannot move how are they able to colonize new areas? Of course they do manage this, and any boat or oil rig that has been in the sea for even a short period is rapidly colonized by seaweeds and a host of sessile animals. This occurs because the majority of marine invertebrates possess a mobile larval stage in their life cycle. Sexual reproduction involves an exchange of sex cells or gametes between two indi-

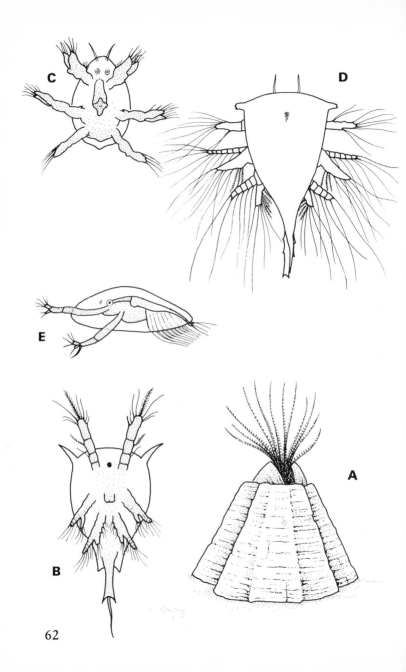

62

viduals and the resulting eggs hatch into a tiny larva, often of microscopic proportions, that usually bears absolutely no similarity to the adult (see, e.g., p. 58). These larvae feed, grow and often metamorphose in the plankton, until a suitable spot to settle on is found. Then a final metamorphoses into the adult form takes place, a change as bizarre as a caterpillar becoming a butterfly. These mobile larvae are of crucial importance in the distribution of sessile species, and though many larvae spend only a few weeks in the open sea, some spend many months and travel thousands of miles.

But even before fertilization can take place, species that cannot meet to exchange gametes in cross fertilization must try to maximize the chance of their gametes joining. Often a form of synchronized spawning occurs when all the individuals in an area release vast amounts of their gametes into the water at exactly the same time, frequently cued by an external environmental influence. This may be a full moon resulting in an exceptionally high tide or a sudden change in water temperature. This method of reproduction occurs in certain worms, mussels and sea urchins. In barnacles this wasteful release of gametes is avoided by one individual fertilizing its neighbour by means of a long extensible penis. To ensure that any two neighbouring barnacles can cross fertilize each other, all individuals possess both male and female sex cells and organs. This hermaphroditism is an important strategy employed by many species in ensuring that any two individuals are able to fertilize each other, thus avoiding the risk of two males or two females meeting and being unable to mate.

The following sections provide information that will help in keeping the animals in the aquarium, giving indications as to feeding for example. But as all aquaria offer slightly different environments some aquarists will succeed with certain species

**Fig. 21** The stages in the life cycle of the barnacle, showing the adult and its microscopic larval forms (not to scale).
**A** The adult with its biramous feeding limbs or cirri extended.
**B C D** Nauplii, the larval form released from the adults, that feed, grow and moult several times whilst in the plankton.
**E** The Cyrpris, the bivalved larva, the final larval stage responsible for selecting the right site to metamorphose into the adult form.

where others, with a basically similar system, will fail. This is partly what makes marine aquarium keeping so fascinating.

## The sponges – Porifera

These are a group of filter feeders, that are not usually easy to introduce into the aquarium. To the casual observer, sponges may not look like or appear to be animals, and some species at a quick glance may not even appear to be living organisms. Sponges are the least complex multi-cellular marine animals. They are totally sessile, and possess neither nervous system nor muscles. Some are solitary individuals carrying on an independent existence, but there are also colonial forms, in which individual organisms are connected with each other, both structurally and physiologically, so that each individual contributes to the whole colony.

The simplest forms of sponges are flask-shaped, with their sides pitted by a multitude of tiny holes, called ostia, so small as to be almost invisible. At the top of the sponge is a much larger hole – the osculum. The body wall has three layers of cells. The outer covering is of rather flat cells, the middle layer contain the skeletal elements of the sponge – the microscopic spicules, the parts that help maintain its form. In the Mediterranean sponge *Spongia officinalis*, the spicules form a skeleton of commercial importance, for when the other tissue is removed the familiar bath sponge is left. The spicules of most sponges are formed of other material – they are often of a calcareous or siliceous nature, and their spiky structure contributes to their protection. Sponges may also be poisonous, and are often brightly coloured – frequently a useful indication that an animal is unpalatable and so should be avoided by possible predators.

The innermost layer of cells of the sponges consist of flagellated cells, whip-like in structure, which beat in synchrony, causing a current of water to flow through the sponge. These cells also catch and ingest tiny food particles that are present in the water – even bacteria may be consumed. Beating flagella are not the only means of drawing the essential food-bearing current of water into the many ostia and out of the osculum. Two other physical phenomena cause a current of water to flow through the sponge.

First is the Venturi effect which makes use of the fact that a current of water moving very close to the surface of the sponge flows at a slower rate than water even a few millimetres further away. The faster current draws water from the osculum which is placed at the top of the sponge. Water is then automatically replaced through the ostia. The Bernoulli effect is another phenomenon utilized by the sponge of the encrusting colonial type. When a current of water flows over their colony it is deflected so that the current is faster at the upper region of the colony and slower lower down. So again water is drawn out of the oscula at the top and replaced via the ostia at the lower region of the colony.

Sponges have remarkable powers of regeneration. In experiments the tissue of certain sponges have been forced through a fine sieve, thus separating the cells, but they soon reorganized to form several new sponges. Sponges may reproduce asexually by vegetative budding or branching, and this is how the colonial forms grow. Specific areas may also break off.

Sponges also reproduce sexually. The sperm and eggs are formed in the middle layer of cells of the body wall. Sponges are hermaphrodite: both male and female sex cells are produced, though often at different times to ensure that self-fertilization does not occur. Fertilization occurs when the sperm from another sponge are drawn into the sponge's body cavity and joins with an egg. A larva is produced that will be free swimming for a short time, until it settles and metamorphoses into the adult form.

Sponges often form associations with other organisms. They may provide a home for worms, brittlestars or various tiny crustacea, which live inside the sponge's body cavity. Sponges are also used for protection and possible camouflage by certain species of crabs. Some sponges grow and engulf the shells of hermit crabs, and some crabs have sponges growing on their bodies and limbs.

*Cliona* is an unusual sponge whose colonies not only cover certain soft rocks and shells, but also bore into them, forming a network of canals filled with the sponge's body. Large sea shells such as oysters often exhibit many tiny holes – the result of this sponge's boring.

Many species of sponge will prove difficult to keep alive in the aquarium if they are introduced as a colony encrusting a rock. Large colonies especially are best avoided because they will not survive in the aquarium and may foul the water as they decompose.

But sponges can survive in the aquarium, including *Cliona*, and though a large colony may not stand being transferred, often a tiny colony or even a larval sponge will develop in the aquarium and grow to form a large mass.

Hydroids and bryozoa are examples of other colonial filter

**Fig. 22** Two species of intertidal sponges. At the top is an encrusting colony of breadcrumb sponges *Halichondria panicea*. Underneath, hanging down from a small ledge, are purse sponges *Grantia compressa*.

feeders that are not easy to transfer to the aquarium. The reason might be to do with their need to adapt to the different conditions found in the aquarium, but if they actually grow up in the aquarium they stand a much better chance of survival.

## Cnidaria

In this phylum there are many species especially suitable for the aquarium. Sea anemones in particular besides being usually not too difficult to find and look after are quite beautiful, often resembling a flower. This phylum also includes the hydroids, jellyfish and corals. These animals exhibit two basic body plans. The first is the polyp – a cylindrical body with the base attached to the substratum, and at the other end a mouth (which also serves as the

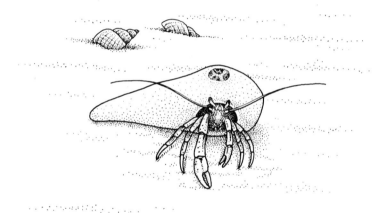

**Fig. 23** The sponge *Suberites domuncula* often grows on shells occupied by hermit crabs. The shell may eventually dissolve away so the crab lives directly inside the sponge. Water enters the sponge through a host of tiny pores all over its complex body mass and is passed out of the large hole, the osculum, clearly visible above the crab's head. Both partners benefit from this symbiotic relationship: the crab gains camouflage and protection, as sponges are distasteful to many organisms; the sponge gains mobility as it is transported to new feeding areas. It is possible that the sponge will not last long in the aquarium, so the crab will be forced to find a new home.

anus), surrounded by a ring of stinging tentacles. Sea anemones are typical polyps – they have soft sac-like bodies, and are common inhabitants of most rocky shores. Corals are polyps which often grow in colonies. The polyp secretes a calcareous external skeleton into which the animal can withdraw. In tropical waters the accumulation of thousands upon thousands of years of coral growth has formed massive coral reefs, and though these reefs do not occur in cooler temperate waters, certain coral species can be found.

The hydroids, which can superficially resemble seaweeds, are also formed from polyps that are colonial, joined together by extensions of their stomach – the cavity inside their cylindrical bodies.

The other body plan of the Cnidaria is the medusa. These are usually free swimming individuals having soft jelly-like, bell-shaped bodies with a ring of pendant tentacles encircling a central mouth. The best-known example of the medusa is the common jellyfish. Some classes of this phylum will have both medusoid and polyp phases in their life cycles.

Cnidarians are radially symmetrical: if cut in half the two parts will be mirror images of each other. Their body wall is made up of two layers of cells separated by a jelly-like layer called the mesoglea. Cnidarians have muscles, and can move – some are very active.

All the members of this phylum are carnivorous, using their tentacles to capture prey, which for smaller species may be tiny planktonic life, or animals such as fish in the case of large jellyfish and anemones. The mechanism of prey capture involves special stinging cells called cnidoblasts unique to this phylum. Each cell contains a nematocyst, a tightly coiled thread, attached to a pear-shaped vesicle, the release of which is triggered by an appropriate stimulus. This is usually a combination of a mechanical stimulus – contact with a potential prey, with a chemical stimulus – which indicates the nature of the prey.

When activated the thread is rapidly discharged, elongating enormously, and in the most common type of nematocyst, pierces the prey, and then acts as a hypodermic needle, injecting poison stored in the vesicle. Other types of nematocysts may release a glue to hold the prey, or release a thread that coils round the prey, entangling it. The poison from the stings of certain tropical jellyfish can kill a man, and even that of some temperate anemones is enough to cause a nasty rash.

There are three main Cnidarian classes – the Hydrozoa, the Scyphozoa and the Anthozoa.

## The Hydrozoa

These are the simplest Cnidarians, most of them belonging to the order Hydroida, the hydroids. They are usually delicately fern-like in growth, less than 1 cm high, and form colonies on rocks, seaweeds or the shells of sea snails or hermit crabs. Their polyps may be specialized for reproduction and defence as well as feeding.

An hydroid's life cycle alternates between a medusoid phase, which reproduces sexually, and a polyp phase, which reproduces asexually. The polyp colony grow by asexual reproduction, but some of the reproductive polyps develop medusae, which then bud off and swim away to be dispersed by the currents and tides. The medusa, like the polyps, is formed from two layers of cells, but most of the body is formed from the mesoglea, giving them a jelly-like consistency.

The medusae swim away from the polyp with a pulsating closing and opening of their bell-shaped bodies, for otherwise they would sink. To serve this active life style the medusae have sensory organs, which detect light and aid in balance, for they must remain in the areas of the sea with the correct amount of light to support their planktonic prey.

The medusae develop gonads in which male and female sex cells are formed. On release of the gametes, fertilization results in the formation of a larva that settles and metamorphoses back into the polyp form. Hydroids will be introduced into the aquarium attached to rocks. It is not usually very easy to keep these filter feeders alive, which may be due to the lack of the right sort of planktonic food.

There are two other smaller orders of this class. The Milleporina usually live in warmer waters, and secrete a hard skeleton of lime, so that they resemble the colonies of true corals.

The Siphonophors are Hydrozoans of the open sea, although winds and currents sweep them into shallow waters, or even wash them ashore. These are free living and form large floating colonies

of both polyps and medusae fused together as a unit. The Portuguese man-o-war *Physalia* is a colony of many different individuals – one functions as a float, and others serve in feeding, digestion and reproduction.

## The Scyphozoa

These are the jellyfish. Their medusoid phase is dominant, but after sexual reproduction a larva is formed that settles on the sea bed and grows into a small polyp phase called the scyphistoma. It buds off many larval jellyfish which grow into the adults.

Most jellyfish inhabit the open sea, and are occasionally washed ashore, but an exception is the stalked jellyfish, whose adults are not free swimming, but live attached to seaweeds and rocks. They are not usually suitable for the aquarium though the species that are not free swimming may be worth trying.

## The Anthozoa

This group includes some of the best-known members of the phylum, among them sea anemones and the corals. They have no medusoid phase in their life cycle – the polyps either reproduce asexually, or sexually when the larva metamorphoses back into a polyp.

Some warm water sea anemones can grow to a diameter of a metre.

Intertidal anemones can change their body shape amazingly. At low tide some expel all the water from their body cavity, and contract to resemble a small blob of jelly, but when re-submerged they take in water through their mouth, pumping it back to their body cavity through two ciliated grooves – the siphonoglyphs. These are situated on the pharynx, which hangs down into the body cavity and acts as a valve preventing the water from escaping. The water sealed inside the anemone acts as an hydrostatic skeleton, for the sets of muscles in the body wall can contract against each other to alter the anemone's shape. For example, if the circular muscles, which run in a continuous layer around the body, are contracted, pressure is built up on the trapped water, and it causes the anemone

**Fig. 24** The sea anemone *Anthopleura* occurs in a variety of colours and often has warts over its column. It is a crevice dweller, sheltering from bright light in the lower regions of the shore.

71

**Fig. 25** The beadlet anemone *Actinia* is shown closed and open. This is a hardy anemone that occurs all over the rocky shore. There are different colour forms: red, green and a red with green spots resembling a strawberry.

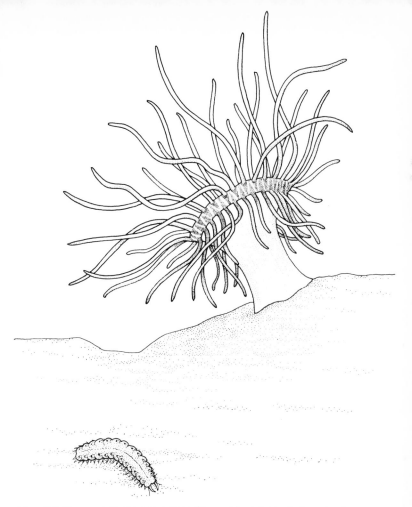

**Fig. 26** The snakelocks anemone, *Anemonia sulcata* thrives in the aquarium and it is best to keep only one small individual. Their long tentacles can give a nasty sting and if well fed they will rapidly increase in size, possibly dividing in two by asexual reproduction.

Some individuals have a greenish hue caused by single-celled algae, called zooxanthellae which live inside the anemone, with both organisms benefiting from the association. These anemones will be seen to bask in bright light.

In the foreground is a small scale worm.

to extend, becoming longer and narrower. Anemones are continuously moving, but these movements are too slow to be appreciated with just a casual glance. Many anemones also have a pedal disc at the base which is used in attachment to the substratum. With these organs, they can slowly crawl. They are not the immobile creatures they initially appear.

In the beadlet anemone, *Actinia*, the base of their stinging tentacles is encircled by a collar of small bumps termed acrorhagi.

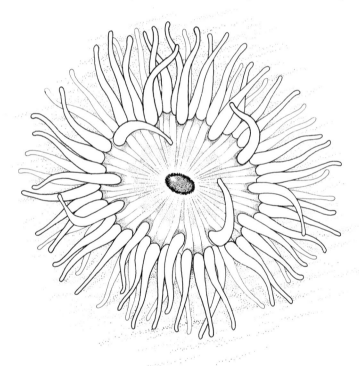

**Fig. 27** The dahlia anemone *Tealia felina* is often found partly buried with its warty column having small shells and stones stuck to it helping in camouflage, especially when closed up. This anemone, like most others, is quite easy to look after in the aquarium. It occurs in a variety of colour forms, some exceptionally beautiful.

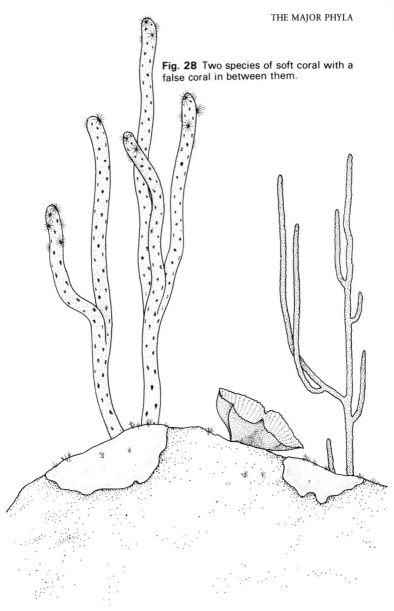

**Fig. 28** Two species of soft coral with a false coral in between them.

These acrorhagi have stinging cells, but rather than being used for prey capture or defence, they are extended and inflated when two beadlet anemones come into contact with each other. In these territorial disputes the vanquished retreats, and it seems that large anemones usually beat smaller ones, and those of the red strain or morph usually defeat those of the green morph. Observations suggest that beadlets that are identical, the result of asexual reproduction, will not fight in this way.

Other species of anemones have formed close relationships with hermit crabs – crabs inhabiting the discarded shells of sea-snails. One of these is *Calliactis* which will, with the crab's help, move on to the crab's shell. This relationship is described as commensalism for both partners benefit – the crab is protected by the anemone's stinging tentacles, and the anemone is transported around by the crab to new food sources, besides eating the crab's leftovers.

Another anemone – *Anemonia* – often exhibits emerald green tentacles. This is because inside its tentacles live algae which have formed a close relationship with the anemone. The algae gain protection and utilize carbon dioxide and other waste products of the anemone's metabolism. The anemone, besides having these substances removed, also gains oxygen – the by-product of the algae's photosynthesis – plus other products manufactured by the algae. Some examples of *Anemonia* lack this algae and appear to exist perfectly well without them.

The true corals belong to the order Madreporia, and though it is in the tropics that corals exist in their most spectacular and impressive forms – the coral reefs – even in cool temperate waters certain species of coral can be found. Each individual coral polyp secretes a hard calcareous skeleton into which it can withdraw. Many of the tropical species are colonial, with the polyps joined together but, although corals of the cooler waters do have colonial forms, it is the solitary species that are most likely to be found, such as *Caryophyllia*.

Anemones and corals are some of the most suitable aquarium inhabitants. Anemones in particular will be found on all shores, and

**Fig. 29** Three tropical Cnidarians. From the top: a colony of zoanthids; a caryophyllid or bubble coral; and two corallimorphs or false corals.

their beauty and variety is quite remarkable. Most species will take small fragments of prawn flesh or some such food so are easy to look after. Most anemones also filter feed. Certain species such as *Actinia* are quite conspicuous but others are burrowers with only their tentacles exposed, so will not be easy to spot. Two or three anemones in the aquarium are usually quite enough. These animals grow to quite large sizes and may live for hundreds of years.

Corals from temperate waters are generally individual forms that are usually never exposed to the air. These forms will survive in the aquarium and can be looked after like the anemones. Tropical corals are often colonial forms that need brightly lit aquaria so the symbiotic algae they often possess can photosynthesize. Many tropical species also filter feed and some may take small fragments of flesh in the aquarium.

Soft corals also occur in temperate and tropical seas. They are not usually found intertidally, but inhabit shallow seas. They are not always easy to keep alive, possibly due to the food, for they are filter feeders, but there may be other reasons. Temperate species may find home aquaria too warm.

## Marine worms

Many people have a preconception of a worm as an ugly, uninteresting little animal. But there are many species, some being ideal for the aquarium, which have a remarkable appearance, with dazzling colours and quite beautiful forms. Many of these different species are found in the sea, and although referred to colloquially as worms, they are not necessarily closely related, belonging to five main phyla.

### Platyhelminthes – the flat worms

The main marine representatives of this phylum (which also contains parasitic flukes and tapeworms) belong to the class Turbellaria. They are free-living, leaf-shaped animals, up to a few centimetres in length. They move about by the combined action of tiny beating hairs on their underside. These cilia, whose numbers may run into thousands, beat in synchrony, enabling the animals to move in an undulating glide. They can use their muscles to change their shape and in some species enable the worm to swim. These worms have developed a primitive brain at their anterior end, a concentration of sensory structures able to detect light or chemicals. Its position at the front of the animal provides information on the environment immediately ahead of it.

Flat worms are bilaterally symmetrical with a definite front and back end, and left and right sides. They have three tissue layers with the middle layer developed to contain organs of excretion and reproduction. There is no hydrostatic skeleton, but the mesoderm forms a simple skeleton on which the muscles can act.

These animals are often hunters, and can extend their pharynx out from their mouths to aid prey capture and the ingestion of food. The gut varies in different species, being either of a simple form or having many branches, and there is no anus.

Flat worms are hermaphrodites, they possess both male and female sex cells. This ensures that mating can take place whenever two worms meet.

Flat worms are not usually particularly suitable aquarium inhabitants as many species are carnivores, feeding on such animals as sea-squirts or bryozoa, and if these fascinating colonial animals are living in the aquarium it is best to avoid keeping flat worms. As there are so many other interesting animals that can safely be kept I prefer to leave them alone.

## Nemertina

These are the proboscis or ribbon worms, a more advanced phylum than the flat worms, and remarkable for the great length to which they can grow – five metres is not unusual. Their bodies are extremely thin and fragile, and they usually remain tightly coiled. They possess a posterior anus so food is taken in at the mouth and travels through the body, being digested before being expelled at the other end.

Their proboscis is not part of the gut but is situated in a special cavity – the rhynchocoel. The proboscis can rapidly be extended to capture prey – usually small worms, and may have jaws or barbs to hold on to the prey. The proboscis is then withdrawn, and the prey transferred to the mouth. Though these worms are not difficult to keep in the aquarium there are disadvantages, as they usually remain hidden and are likely to eat any other worm in the tank.

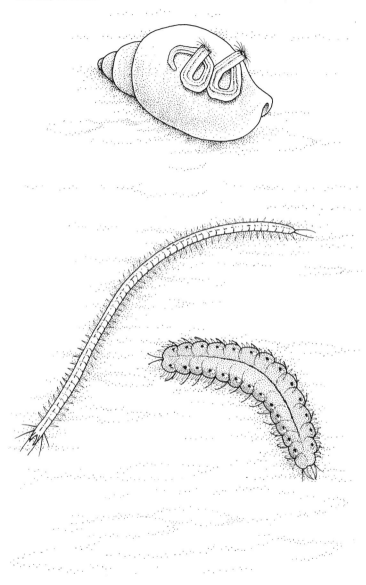

## Annelida

These segmented worms have bodies which are divided into a number of clearly defined repeating units. They have a hydrostatic skeleton with well-developed longitudinal and circular muscles, often a head with sensory organs, and each body segment usually bears bristles called chaetae.

There are three major Annelid classes – the Oligochaeta which include the earthworms with few marine representatives; the Hirudinae – the leeches; and finally the Polychaeta, with many diverse marine species and forms.

## The Polychaeta

These worms usually have a head with antennae, eyes and jaws. Each of the repeating segments that make up the rest of their bodies has a pair of lobes on either side which are the parapodia that usually assist in locomotion. The lobes bear the bristles or chaetae which give the group its name.

Beside the gut running through the centre of their bodies, with an anterior mouth and a posterior anus, there is also another body cavity called the coelom which surrounds the gut. This coelom is fluid-filled and forms the basis of the hydrostatic skeleton. The segmentation of the body permits each unit to act independently, resulting in great flexibility in movement.

Most polychaete individuals are of single sex and fertilization is external with the gametes shed into the water. To limit the waste involved in this method an external event is often utilized as a stimulus. This synchronized spawning, when all the gametes are shed, can be cued by such things as day length, temperature changes, or a full moon with its resulting influence on the tides.

Another method of ensuring synchrony is for the first gametes

**Fig. 30** There are three types of polychaete worm, that can all be found on rocky shores and should be all right in the aquarium.

At the top are the serpulid or tube worms *Hydroides norvegica*, that live in chalky tubes attached to rocks or shells. These worms are filter feeders.

In the middle is *Nereis* a rag worm, that plays a useful role in the aquarium as a scavenger. On the shore it is usually found under rocks or burrowing in softer sediments.

At the bottom is *Hermione hystrix*, a scale worm, also a useful scavenger in the tank.

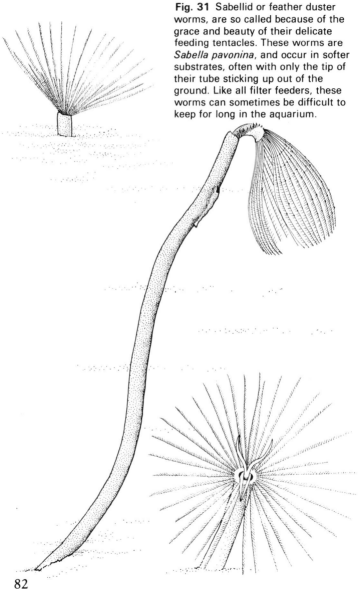

**Fig. 31** Sabellid or feather duster worms, are so called because of the grace and beauty of their delicate feeding tentacles. These worms are *Sabella pavonina*, and occur in softer substrates, often with only the tip of their tube sticking up out of the ground. Like all filter feeders, these worms can sometimes be difficult to keep for long in the aquarium.

released to stimulate the release of gametes from other individuals cued by some hormone they contain.

Some nereid worms undergo a change in their body form prior to spawning, whereby the parapodia develop into paddle-like appendages used to help them swim up to the surface.

Polychaetes divide into two main groups, the errant and the sedentary. Errant polychaetes have a free-living life style actively moving about in search of prey. Their heads are usually armed with an array of sensory organs – eyes, palps, tentacles and there may be a proboscis, an organ that can be extended out of the mouth to capture prey. Many of these worms will be ideal aquarium inhabitants serving as scavengers cleaning up the leftovers of other creatures. There are scale worms such as hermione, with rows of scales down their backs resembling armour plate, or small delicate syllid worms. Two other groups likely to be encountered are the nereids and the paddleworms. All of these worms will actively scavenge around the aquarium and some are of dazzling colours – bright greens, reds or irridescent hues.

The second category, the sedentary polychaetes, live in tubes or burrows. As they do not have such an active life style they have not evolved so many of the sensory structures of the errant varieties, but there is always a highly developed food gathering apparatus. One especially common group are the serpulids whose tiny white chalky tubes which protect the worm's body, occur on rocks and the fronds of seaweeds. From this tube the worm can extend a delicate and beautiful crown of tentacles into the water. This structure acts as a sieve that traps food particles that are then transferred to the mouth in the centre of the crown. The sabellids are similar types of worms though often larger, with their tubes formed from sand or mud. Both these types of worm will survive in the aquarium especially if regular water changes with natural seawater provide plenty of plankton. In these worms the tentacles are also used for respiration and in some cases one may be modified to form an operculum – a plug that blocks the tube after the worm has withdrawn inside.

Another group of sedentary polychaetes are the terebellids whose soft bodies usually lie protected in crevices or holes. These worms possess a multitude of tentacles, often many centimetres in length. These tentacles rove about and when food particles are encountered on the sea floor they are ensnared and passed back to the worm's mouth. This method of feeding is known as deposit feeding. *Amphitrite* is an example of this group.

### Echiuroidea

These worms have a sac-like body with a proboscis that can extend to rove over the substrate to collect detritus.

Usually the worm found is the female, which may be around 10 centimetres in length. The male is a tiny parasite living on her body.

### Sipunculoidea - the peanut worms

These worms get their common name from their body shape. They have an extensible proboscis, with a mouth at the end, which is surrounded by a ring of frilly tentacles. They eat detritus, a popular food source for many worms, and they often live in silty crevices or under rocks.

Worms from these two phyla may be brought back with rocks from the shore, and they will probably be perfectly healthy feeding on any scraps and leftovers they may find.

## Crustacea

Though older texts may refer to the crustaceans as part of a larger phylum, the Arthropoda, zoologists now give these animals separate phylum status. Crustaceans include the crabs, lobsters and prawns, and many tiny species which live their whole lives as part of the plankton. Most crustaceans are marine, but some live in freshwater, and there are terrestrial representatives, such as wood lice. The barnacles, which are so familiar and abundant on rocky shores, are also crustaceans.

All crustaceans have a hard external skeleton, formed from a substance called chitin and strengthened by calcium salts, which gives protection against predators, and provides support for the body. In many species, it is clearly segmented to allow flexibility at the joints. The body is divided into three main regions: the head, the thorax and the abdomen. The head bears two antennae and the mouth parts. In some species there are also compound eyes, and an aggregation of nerve cells that form a brain. The head is often enclosed by the carapace, an outgrowth of the skeleton, that forms a protective fused unit. There are paired limbs on the thorax and abdomen. These are usually jointed and perform a variety of functions according to the life style of the particular species. The legs of the thorax may be the walking legs, and the legs of the abdomen the swimming legs.

The crustacean 'armour plating' provides many benefits, but it creates a problem: in order to increase in size the animal must split open its old skeleton and shed it, in a process called ecdysis. After a rapid period of growth, a new skeleton is formed. Meanwhile, the crustacean is vulnerable and may seek a sheltered place for its moult until the newly formed skeleton hardens.

There are eight crustacean classes, but only two are especially relevant here: the Cirripedia (the barnacles), and the Malacostraca (the crabs and prawns).

## Cirripedia - the barnacles

Barnacles start their lives in the same way as most crustaceans, as a free-swimming planktonic larvae. The larva is called a nauplius, but soon metamorphoses into another entirely different larval form called a cypris. The cypris larva is highly modified to find exactly the right site to settle to undergo its final metamorphoses into adult form. Barnacles are sessile organisms, and once attached cannot change their position, so it is crucial for the cypris to choose a favourable spot – it cannot change its decision. However, it can land repeatedly, even on exposed, wave-beaten rocks, and investigate each site testing for currents, light and surface texture. The presence of other members of its species is also important, for they provide a positive indication that the site is suitable for settlement.

On metamorphoses, the cement glands firmly attach the anterior end of the barnacle to the rocks. The adult bears little resemblance to more typical crustaceans. It lacks sensory antennae and compound eyes and its abdomen is greatly reduced in size, with the segmentation typical of most crustaceans very indistinct. The whole animal is protected by a carapace, and reinforced by a number of calcareous plates (which provide the best way to identify the barnacle species). Six pairs of limbs are attached to the barnacle's thorax; these 'cirri' are periodically extended from the protective shell to comb the water, for the barnacles are filter feeders, sieving planktonic life for nutriment.

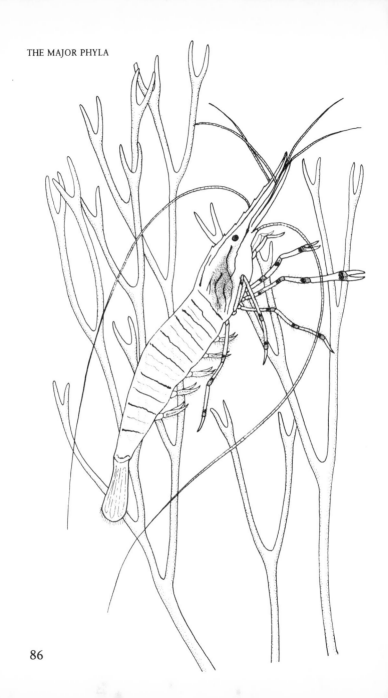

Barnacles are hermaphrodites and cross fertilization takes place by means of an extensible penis that is long enough to introduce sperm into the neighbouring barnacles. The acorn barnacles *Balanus* are well known, for they occur in vast numbers on many rocky shores. There are also parasitic species such as *Sacculina* which infects certain crabs.

Barnacles are filter feeders and so regular water changes will help them in the aquarium, though they are not the easiest of animals to keep alive. It might possibly be that many species are used to being left high and dry for some of the time when the tide goes out, or they require the plankton and oxygen-rich water that comes in with the waves of the flowing tide. If the conditions in the aquarium are very tranquil barnacles used to being continually submerged, in rock pools for example, may possibly do better.

## The Malacostraca

The largest and most diverse crustacean class is typified by the prawn, with its stalked compound eyes, carapace, enclosed head and thorax, and limbs adapted for food gathering, walking and swimming. The thoracic limbs have the gills at their base, and in females are used to carry their fertilized eggs.

The Isopoda order includes representatives resembling wood lice in their very flat bodies which lack a carapace. One isopod, *Ligia*, lives right at the top of the intestidal zone, feeding at night on decaying seaweed. These will never do well in the aquarium.

The Amphipods are bound to be introduced with rocks and weeds. It is quite likely some will survive and even breed in the tank. Amphipods are often laterally flattened and so crawl along on their sides. Jumping legs may be present on the abdomen, for some species can leap about. The male is often larger than the female, and they may move about with the male holding the female prior to mating.

The Decapoda order includes the crabs and prawns. In these best-known crustaceans the head and thorax are fixed together and covered by a carapace. There are eight pairs of limbs on the thorax, the first three reduced in size to form mouthparts, the other five

**Fig. 32** The common prawn *Leander serratus*, is an active and hardy animal that will do well in the aquarium.

87

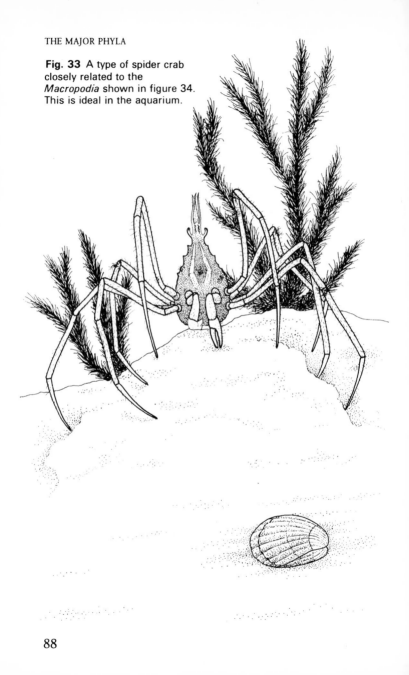

**Fig. 33** A type of spider crab closely related to the *Macropodia* shown in figure 34. This is ideal in the aquarium.

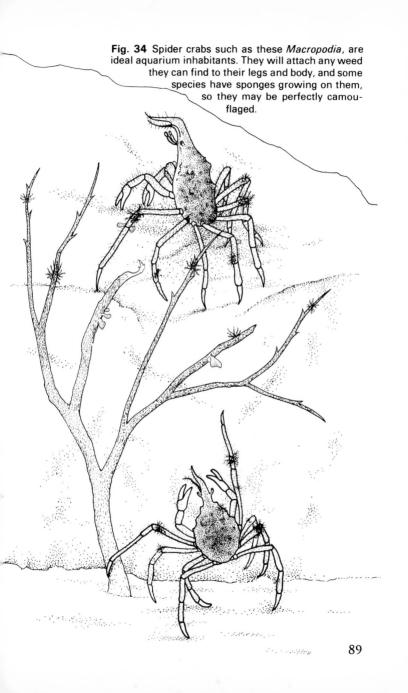

**Fig. 34** Spider crabs such as these *Macropodia*, are ideal aquarium inhabitants. They will attach any weed they can find to their legs and body, and some species have sponges growing on them, so they may be perfectly camouflaged.

form walking legs. This order is divided into two main groups – the swimmers, Natantia, such as prawns; and the crawlers, Reptantia, such as crabs and lobsters. Both groups have representatives that are highly suitable for the marine aquarium.

The Natantians generally have a light exoskeleton with the abdomen bearing paddle-like swimming limbs. Many species can change their colour rapidly. This is made possible by the presence of chromatophores, cells containing pigments that can either be expanded to expose more colour, or contracted to become almost invisible, making the animal virtually transparent.

In many species of prawn the male fertilizes the female soon after her moult, when her exoskeleton is still soft. A clump of up to 3,000 eggs develops under the female's abdomen. On hatching a planktonic zoea larva is released, for the nauplius stage of the larva is completed within the egg. Prawns are some of the easiest animals to keep. Besides being quite fascinating to watch they are useful scavengers helping to keep the tank clean.

The skeleton of Reptantians is generally very strong and heavy. There are often robust walking legs on the thorax, with the first pair forming conspicuous pincers. In the lobsters the segmented abdomen bears paddle-like limbs.

Hermit crabs have adapted to living in the discarded shell of various species of gastropod. The soft vulnerable abdomen has evolved to fit into the spiral shells, and often one of the pincers is larger than the other, and serves to block the mouth of the shell after the hermit has retreated inside. Hermit crabs often support a miniature ecosystem associated with their shells, and this applies particularly to the larger individuals. Often tube worms, sponges or hydroids may grow on the shell. Some species of anemone live in association with hermit crabs, and other animals, such as bristle worms, isopods and porcelain crabs, may live inside the shell. Hermit crabs are ideal aquarium inhabitants, as they are easy to feed and also pick up the leftovers of others. It is quite fascinating to observe the semaphore-like signals they constantly send out using their mouth parts, and also to watch them change their shell

**Fig. 35** Hairy crabs *Pilumnus hirtellus*, are small crevice-dwelling crabs found in the lower regions of the shore. They are quite suitable for the aquarium.

91

**Fig. 36** This is another type of spider crab, *Hyas*, and though quite suitable for the aquarium, larger specimens should be avoided as they will lumber clumsily around the tank disturbing other organisms.

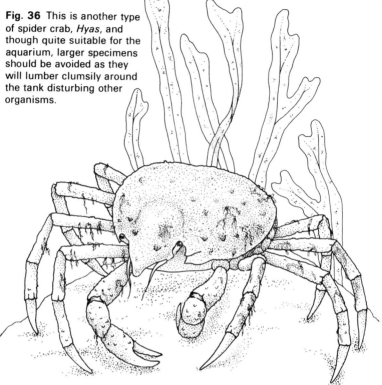

when they find an empty one. For those that have an anemone on their shell, after the crab has moved out it then helps the anemone hop over too.

Porcelain crabs are close relatives of the hermit crabs and are more commonly found in silty crevices where they filter feed. Often they appear quite hairy. Their common name derives from the tendency of their limbs to break off easily.

The true crabs have a characteristically strong flat circular carapace, with the abdomen greatly reduced in size and tucked underneath the body.

Some species of crabs rove pugnaciously around the shore feeding on any animal matter they can grab. These species, such as the shore crab, swimming crab or edible crab are not suitable for the aquarium as they will adversely affect other animals; even small ones cause problems. Other species live quieter lives: some spider crabs, for example, cover themselves with weeds or sponges

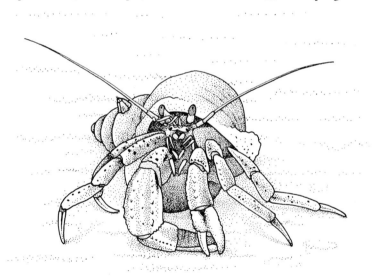

**Fig. 37** The hermit crab *Eupagurus bernhardus* is a fascinting animal to keep in the aquarium, and it also plays a useful role in cleaning up. Its shell often supports a miniature ecosystem of encrusting organisms.

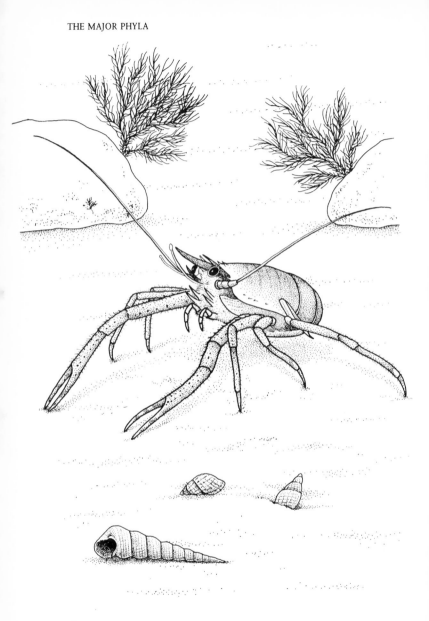

and remain perfectly camouflaged to avoid predators, and to surprise their own prey. Another species – the pea crab, lives inside the mantle cavity of bivalves such as mussels or oysters. The female of the species often grows much larger than the male, and develops a thin soft shell, for she needs no extra protection within the mollusc's shell. These types of crab are much better suited for the aquarium.

## Mollusca

This is a huge phylum including such diverse members as slugs, snails, mussels and squid. Most people think of a shell as the obvious molluscan characteristic, but there are molluscs with tiny internal shells, and some with no shells at all.

Molluscs are soft-bodied creatures, with a bilaterally symmetrical unsegmented body. Many have bodies that can be clearly divided into a head, which may have the mouth and sensory organs, a foot for locomotion, and a visceral mass containing the gut and other internal organs.

A sheath of skin called a mantle often cloaks part of the body, and it may secrete the shell, or provide a cavity for the gills. Unlike the gills of most animals those of molluscs are covered with tiny beating hairs called cilia, that help drive a current of water over their surface.

The molluscan shell is made up of three layers: an outer layer – the periostracum, formed of protein; a middle prismatic layer of calcium carbonate; and an inner mother-of-pearl lining – the nacreous layer. The nacreous layer is used to repair fractures in the shell, or in some cases to coat foreign bodies and form a pearl.

There are four classes of mollusc that are likely to be found on the rocky shore, though the group that includes the octopus, squid and cuttlefish will be encountered only rarely.

*Polyplacophora - the chitons*

The chitons, or coat-of-mail shells are rather inconspicuous

**Fig. 38** Squat lobsters are fascinating aquarium inhabitants, this one is *Munida rugosa*, a deep water species. Its inter-tidal relatives live in crevices and under rocks on the lower regions of the shore. In the foreground are two whelks and an empty turret shell.

95

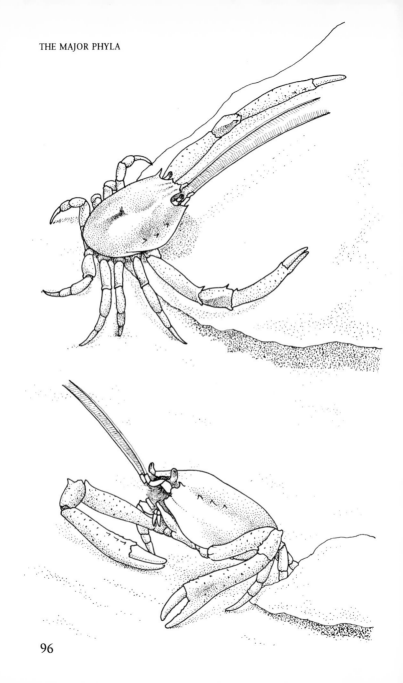

creatures, often dark in colour, which cling tenaciously to the underside of rocks and boulders. No more than a few centimetres in length their elliptically shaped bodies are composed of eight linked plates – hence their common name.

A chiton's anterior head, hidden beneath its shell, lacks eyes and sensory tentacles, but chitons do have eyes in large numbers on their dorsal surface. These eyes, which penetrate the shell, are very small and of complex design.

Chitons are grazers. They scrape algae off the rocks with a special organ, the radula. This is a band of teeth which are constantly being renewed. As the scraping teeth are worn down new teeth come forward to replace them.

Chitons shed eggs or sperm into the water: fertilization is external. The resulting trochophore larvae resembles that of the polychaetes. The foot, which is responsible for the chitons' strong grip on the rocks, takes up the whole of the underside of the animal. It grips by adhesion – not suction – for the chiton secretes a thin layer of mucus that actually sticks the animal to the rock. Chitons are perfectly suitable for the aquarium, though as for all grazing herbivores, the aquarium must support the algae that forms a thin layer over the rocks and glass as most adequately lit aquaria do.

## Gastropoda - snails

The gastropods form the largest molluscan class, including top shells, limpets, cowries and the slugs. Many of this group have managed to colonize land, but most gastropods (and indeed most molluscs) are aquatic.

Many gastropods possess a spiral shell though in the sea-slugs the passive, physical protection the shell offers is replaced by an adaptation of the skin, which secretes chemicals to deter predators, and produces colours as camouflage or in some cases very bright hues, to advertize the slug as unpleasant to bite. The gastropods are divided into two main sub-classes, the Prosobranchia – the sea-snails – and the Opistobranchia – the sea-slugs.

**Fig. 39** The masked crab *Corystes cassivelaunus* is usually found buried in sand. Its long antennae form a tube through which water is drawn to reach the gills whilst the animal is buried. It usually does well in the aquarium.

*Prosobranchia* are characterized by the way in which their visceral mass, the gut and other internal organs, are coiled in a tight spire to fit into the shell. In common with all gastropods, their primary stage is a trochophore larva, but this soon metamorphoses into a veliger. The veliger has a tiny shell enclosing the visceral mass, a foot and also a velum, a delicate flap covered with cilia that aids in locomotion and feeding. At one stage in their evolution as the veliger swam through the water its velum hung down conspicuously, but when danger threatened, in the form of one of the numerous planktonic predators, such as arrow worms, it pulled its foot and then its velum into its shell. This state of affairs gradually changed for the visceral mass enclosed within the shell underwent a twisting of 180°. This meant that the space into which the foot and the velum were drawn into – the mantle cavity – was now placed so that when danger threatened the velum was drawn in first, then the foot. This is advantageous to the veliger, because the foot then served to protect the entrance of the shell, and the delicate organs within. This twisting is known as torsion, and as a result when the veliger metamorphoses into the adult, the twisted visceral mass remains in its position, and so does the mantle cavity. This leaves the structures in the mantle cavity – the anus, the gills and a pair of sensory osphradia – at the front of the animal, just above its head. Having the sensory and respiratory organs at the anterior end is useful in gaining information on the water ahead, but the animal must also ensure that this important area is not fouled by its own waste products. Keyhole limpets have a hole in their shell to expel their waste – and in other limpet species the gills are situated surrounding the foot. Many other species have a gill on only one side of the cavity, with the anus on the other: water is drawn in on the gills' side and expelled on the opposite side, taking waste products with it.

Many prosobranch gastropods, such as limpets, winkles or topshells, are herbivores, which use their radulae to scrape algae off rocks and stones. Others, such as whelks and cowries, are carnivores. Certain whelks bore holes into the shells of mussels,

**Fig. 40** A species of rather pugnacious shore crab, the type best left alone by the marine aquarist.

and some cowries eat colonial tunicates. In tropical waters species of cone shell exist, which have their radulae modified to act like poison darts which can be forced into prey by their extensible proboscis. Some cone shells are highly specialized, and prey upon specific items such as worms, other snails or even fish. In cooler temperate waters such a degree of specialization does not occur and predatory gastropods, such as whelks, are adapted to deal with a variety of different food items. This is because the rapidly changing seasonal regime of the temperate zones makes conditions subject to fluctuation. From summer to winter, certain prey items may not be available, so a 'generalist' has a better chance of survival.

Reproduction in prosobranchs may involve the shedding of gametes into the water – external fertilization. This occurs in limpets, for example, but in the more advanced species such as whelks, internal fertilization occurs after two individuals join in copulation. Top shells, edible periwinkles and limpets are examples of grazers and a small tank will probably be able to support two or three. Whelks are scavengers and may also prey on barnacles and mussels. Other snails, such as cowries, will survive in the aquarium if their specific food is available. For the British cowrie it is certain Ascidians.

*Opisthobranchia* are most typically characterized by the sea-slugs, which lack a shell, mantle cavity and osphradia although some members of this sub-class do possess a shell. One group of opisthobranchs, the nudibranchs, is especially beautiful, often

**Fig. 41** A selection of molluscs.
At the top is a *Murex* from the Mediterranean. This is a close relative of the whelks, and will feed on scraps of prawn meat or will bore into mussels if it gets the chance.

Below is a top shell *Gibula* and two edible periwinkles *Littorina littorea*. These are grazing herbivores and will survive in an aquarium that supports a good growth of micro algae over the rocks and glass.

At the bottom are three netted dog whelks *Nassarius reticulatus* and a common cockle *Cerastoderma*. The whelks are generally found just under the surface of sandy areas of the shore with their long siphons protruding, constantly testing the water for the scent of food. In the aquarium they are useful scavengers. The cockle is also a burrower into softer sediments, and usually all that can be seen of it are its two siphons, one for drawing water in and the other for expelling it after filter feeding.

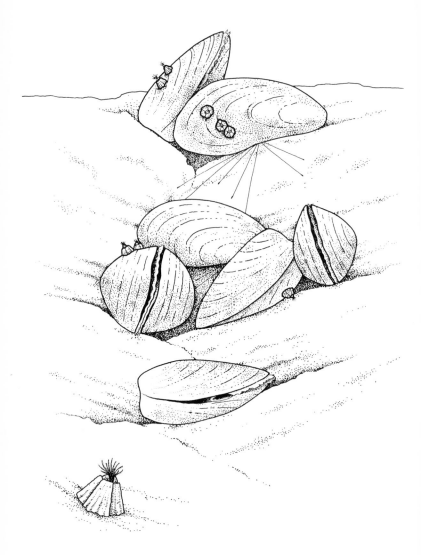

displaying a variety of colours to dazzling effect. Some species bear a mass of tiny tubular appendages on their dorsal surface, and if the sea-slug feeds on anemones, it may store the anemones stinging cells in these 'cerata' for its own defence. There are also species of sea-slug – such as *Elysia* – that feed on algae, and rather than digest the plants' chloroplasts (the site of photosynthesis, the energy manufacturing process of plants) it stores them undamaged, and uses them to its own advantage.

In this group the torsion of the veliger at the larvae stage is reversed later in the life cycle. It is not understood exactly why gastropod larvae undergo torsion, and even less so why detorsion occurs in the opisthobranchs.

Though dazzling sea inhabitants, the highly specific food of certain sea-slugs makes them unsuitable for keeping in an aquarium. Many have comparatively short lives and so unless it is known what a sea-slug eats and a good supply of the food is available it is best not to collect these animals.

## Bivalvia – the bivalves

Bivalves include mussels, scallops and oysters. Their shells have two separate plates or valves hinged by a ligament. In most bivalves, the head, with its tentacles and radula, is missing, for although many species do have limited powers of locomotion, they maintain a fairly sessile life style. Most bivalves are filter feeders, drawing in seawater to sieving out its nutrient content, such as plankton.

The mussel *Mytilus* is a typical bivalve, often found in large numbers on rocky shores. Like all bivalves, it has a foot, but it does not use it in the same way as a slug or a snail. On the foot is a gland

**Fig. 42** Mussels are bivalve molluscs that usually do well in the aquarium, and they may be considered as beneficial natural filters. Mussels are also a food for carnivores such as certain species of whelks or starfish. A large clump of mussels often has a host of associated species including barnacles, bryozoa and worms. Their life cycle involves the production of millions of tiny larvae. A small proportion become young mussels which grow attached to weeds in deeper offshore waters. If they were to join the large mussels too soon they could well be eaten. When they reach a suitable size they allow the waves and currents to carry them to the mussel beds where they anchor themselves with their fine byssus threads.

that secretes a liquid that soon hardens to form a thread called byssus. These threads are used to anchor the mussel to rocks, or other mussels, and with them the mussel can actually haul itself along. Mussels may be found on shores which have to take a considerable wave battering – a testimony to the strength of their byssus threads.

Reproduction as in all bivalves involves external fertilization, whereby the gametes are shed into the water. The resulting trochophore larvae metamorphose into veligers before they settle out of the plankton to change into the adult form. There is always a slim chance that filter feeders with planktonic larval forms may actually consume their own offspring, but tides, currents and the sheer weight of numbers, makes it likely that the larvae will be dispersed (and then probably consumed elsewhere).

Mussels live attached to rocks, but the piddock *Pholas* is a bivalve that actually bores a hole into the rock and lives protected by its burrow. These animals, along with other burrowing species such as sponges, can form a component of erosion as their activity gradually weakens the rocks until it crumbles. Then of course the bivalve will fall out and probably be eaten in its vulnerable state, but the newly exposed area of rock will be a site for their larvae to settle and start the cycle again. The piddock has a serrated edge on the parts of its shell in contact with the rock, and using its muscular foot to grip, it rasps away, thus extending its burrow. It also has a long siphon that extends right up to the opening of its hole, which may be over 20 cm long, with which it draws in the water for its filter feeding. Mussels usually do well in the aquarium, and when gathered in a clump a host of other organisms will be introduced with them. Most bivalves are worth trying though scallops and oysters never seem to last long, possibly there is not enough plankton for them in the aquarium.

## Cephalopoda

This molluscan class, which includes the squids, octopus and cuttlefish is often described as the zenith of invertebrate evolution. The head and the foot are fused together to give a body plan with the head and a mouth surrounded by suckered tentacles at one end, and the visceral mass at the other.

Cephalopods have internal shells which they use to control their

**Fig. 43** The lesser octopus *Eledone
cirrhosa*, is like all cephalopods a
beautiful and intelligent animal. It should
only be kept by more experienced marine
aquarists with large well-maintained
aquaria. In the foreground is a netted dog
whelk.

105

buoyancy. They move by jet propulsion, forcibly ejecting water from their mantle cavity, and have become free-swimming predators. Their prey includes crabs, lobsters, prawns and fish. Some deep-sea squids may exceed 25 m in length, and they are the fastest swimming marine animals.

But it is the nervous system of the cephalopods that makes them the most highly developed invertebrates. Octopuses have been shown to have a learning capacity, and the cephalopod eye has evolved to resemble and function in a remarkably similar way to that of vertebrates. It is ironical that the cephalopods, the most highly developed invertebrates are a declining group, from the evolutionary point of view. The fossil record shows that there were many thousands of forms, now sadly extinct – ammonites are the best known of these. But today there are only 400 species.

Reproduction in cephalopods involves the male transferring sperm to the female after courtship. Eggs are soon laid, and guarded by the female in the case of octopuses. There are no pelagic larvae for the whole development takes place in the egg and a fully formed adult hatches out. Certain cephalopods, such as small octopuses, will live in the aquarium but generally this group is best left alone, or only attempted by the more experienced aquarist.

## Bryozoa

This phylum consists of tiny sessile animals which form colonies of remarkable geometric precision and beauty. They are exceedingly common on rocky shores, growing on rocks, stones, seaweeds and mollusc shells. Though on the shore the colonies most often found are flat and encrusting, there are bryozoan colonies which resemble corals, seaweeds or hydroids. Growing in a colonial form provides many benefits to a species. Not only may it grow in different directions at once, so maximizing its use of space and resources, but if part of the colony is attacked or dies off, the rest of the colony can carry on growing. The colony starts with one individual dividing in half by asexual reproduction. It is by these divisions constantly repeated that the colony increases in size.

A typical bryozoan is *Membranipora* whose colonies encrust

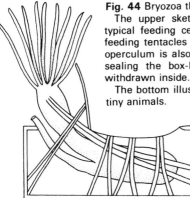

**Fig. 44** Bryozoa through a hand lens.

The upper sketch is a cross-section of one typical feeding cell or zoid. The lophophore of feeding tentacles is extended. The trapdoor-like operculum is also clearly visible. It shuts down sealing the box-like cell if the tentacles are withdrawn inside.

The bottom illustration is of a colony of these tiny animals.

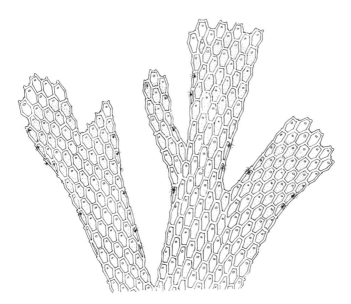

**Fig. 45** The crinoid or feather star *Antedon bifida* is a beautiful but delicate filter feeder of the sublittoral zone. It is not encountered very often, but if found it can survive in the aquarium.

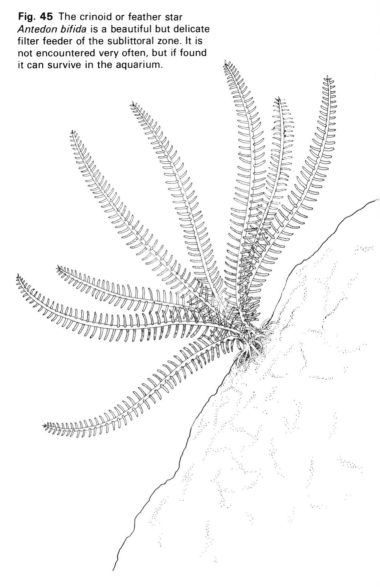

seaweeds, and each cell, best seen with the aid of a magnifying glass, is the skeletal box called a zooecium in which lives one individual – called a zoid. Polymorphic individuals exist in each colony, some are responsible for feeding, some for protection and some for keeping the colony silt free. The feeding zoids are called autozooids and when a protective operculum is raised a ring of tentacles is extended that is responsible for filter feeding. Other zoids called avicularia resemble birds' beaks. Their pecking action deters certain predators, or overgrowth from another colonial form. The zoids responsible for preventing the colony silting up, and also for maintaining a circulation of water over the colony, are called vibracula. The zoids of each colony are connected by pores in the wall of the zooecium, so nutrients can be passed round the colony. Though the colony increases in size by asexual reproduction, sexual reproduction results in a free-swimming planktonic larvae that will settle to form a new colony.

Bryozoa are one of the many encrusting organisms introduced with rocks and in the aquarium may not always do well. It is possible for them to thrive, with their colonies expanding and even growing over the sides of the tank. This is most likely to happen when regular water changes with natural seawater take place, for their larvae may be introduced as well as supplying food for the filter-feeding adults. But these are just one of the organisms which may exist in one aquarium when another apparently similar tank will not support them. It is just one of the challenges constantly confronting the marine aquarist.

## Echinodermata

This phylum includes the starfish, sea-urchins and sea-cucumbers as its members. Many texts on the echinoderm often refer to their 'uniqueness'. Of course, by definition, all animal phyla are unique, but there are many characteristics that are exclusive to this group in symmetry, structure, form and function.

Echinoderms are radially symmetrical with no distinct head region. This is clearly seen in the globular sea-urchins. They also have a penta-radial symmetry, with the body divided into five or more distinct rays. Starfish are obvious examples, but the urchins, too, have five distinct bands on their surface.

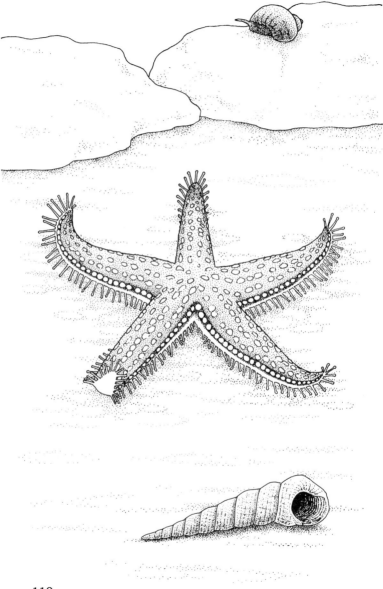

The echinoderm skeleton is internal, usually covered with a thin layer of cells, pierced, in the case of some starfish and sea-urchins, by spines. It consists of many plates of calcium carbonate, joined by collagen fibres. This forms a pliant network that may give a degree of flexibility, or form a solid shell or 'test' as in the case of sea-urchins.

Another unique echinoderm characteristic is the water vascular system, manifested on the outside of the body by rows of tube-feet. These usually occur in five rows extending down each body ray. Pressure within the body can extend a tube foot by filling it with fluid. Each tube foot has longitudinal muscles which not only allow it to bend, so step-like locomotry movements can occur, but when the tube foot is not being used, the muscles can contract withdrawing it back into the body. When this happens a tube foot can automatically be extended somewhere else with no extra energy being required.

Sea-urchins, sea-cucumbers and some starfish have suckers on the ends of their tube feet. This system is sensitive to the pressure outside the animal's body. If the pressure is increased, for example, by the depth of water rising as the tide comes in, the water pressure generated inside the animal may not be enough to extend the tube feet. So there exists a valve, called a madreporite, which serves in equilibrating outside and internal pressures by either taking in or releasing water.

There are five main groups of echinoderms – *Crinoidea*, the feather stars; *Asteroidea*, the starfishes; *Ophiuroidea*, the brittle stars; *Echinoidea*, the sea-urchins and *Holothuroidea*, the sea-cucumbers.

The starfish and urchins have their mouths on their undersides, the oral surface and their anus on the opposite side, the aboral surface. The oral surface is uppermost in the feather stars and the anus too is on this side. Brittle stars possess a mouth on their underside, and this also functions as the anus. In the sea-cucumbers the mouth and anus are at opposite ends of the animal's long worm-like body.

**Fig. 46** *Astropecten irregularis*, a burrowing starfish of the softer sediments. This is a suitable species for the aquarium and is quite easy to feed.

Feather stars are the simplest echinoderms. Segmented hooked limbs called cirri are used to attach their small bodies to the rocks, and though rare on any rocky shore, these animals may be found in pools right at the lowest limits of the shore. The arms of feather stars are long delicate structures that are wafted in the water in filter feeding. They may be broken due to their fragile nature, but can regrow, and also in certain circumstances enable the feather star to swim by undulating in a graceful sinuous movement. These animals are not easy to keep for long in the aquarium, possibly due to the lack of the right sort of food.

The starfish are well-known inhabitants of the shore. Their body is generally formed of five or more stout arms or rays, each bearing rows of tube feet on the oral surface. The madreporite and anus are on the aboral surface. The body surface may be armoured by plates or ossicles. Pedicellariae also exist. These are minute pincer-like organs used in the cleaning and maintenance of the body surface, and in discouraging the settlement of the larvae of certain fouling organisms. The limbs of starfish can be regenerated and some species may actually reproduce by splitting in half.

Different species of starfish have different food preferences. *Marthasterias* is a molluscivore, choosing mussels or winkles. It can use its suckered tube feet to pull apart the shells of the bivalves, and then inserts its stomach into the mussel to digest the flesh. There are many starfish that thrive in the aquarium, *Astropecten* and *Luidia* are just two. They are fairly easy to feed, on scraps of prawn meat for example, and also act as scavengers. Some starfish are voracious predators on other aquarium inhabitants, as they can extend their stomachs to engulf and digest their prey. For this reason only keep small cushion stars. *Henricia* is one starfish that never seems to do well in the tank.

Brittle stars have a body, or central disc sharply separated from the five thin spiny arms. The tube feet have no suckers, for

**Fig. 47** The spiny starfish *Marthasterias glacialis* is another suitable aquarium species. It feeds on scraps of flesh plus molluscs such as winkles or mussels, so if one wants to keep such organisms leave these starfish alone. It is found under rocks and boulders on the lower regions of the shore. Its conspicuous spines are surrounded by rings of small pincer-like pedicellariae, best seen with a magnifying glass.

113

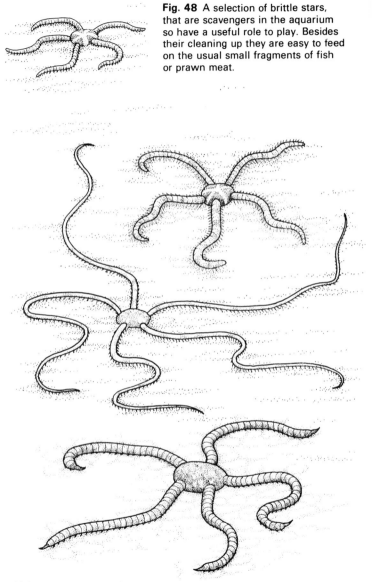

**Fig. 48** A selection of brittle stars, that are scavengers in the aquarium so have a useful role to play. Besides their cleaning up they are easy to feed on the usual small fragments of fish or prawn meat.

locomotion occurs by rapid snake-like flexing of the arms. The tube feet are used in feeding by producing a sticky mucus that adheres to food particles that are then transferred from one tube foot to the other, and finally to the mouth. Most brittle stars are detritivores, feeding on dead or decaying scraps of organic matter; for this reason they are ideal aquarium inhabitants. They are usually found sheltering under rocks and stones, or in crevices, lower down the shore.

Sea-urchins are usually spherical, though there are species with either flattened or oval bodies. Through their test, their calcium carbonate skeleton, protrude five separate double rows of tube feet. The tube feet are only used in locomotion, and there are spines that may also assist in locomotion. The spines are attached to tubercles on the test, ball and socket joints, which give the spine a wide range of movement.

The mouth of sea-urchins is in the form of a complex chewing apparatus known as 'Aristotle's lantern', due to its resemblance to a Greek five-sided lantern. Most sea-urchins are herbivores, grazing on various types of algae, though some species will rasp off a variety of encrusting organisms.

The spines of sea-urchins can be quite sophisticated in some species, such as the burrowing heart-urchins, though the species found on rocky shores generally have more simple spines. But all sea-urchins possess pedecellariae, that are used in keeping the test clear of debris or fouling organisms. The pedecellariae of sea-urchins are much more sophisticated than those of the starfish, and are of four main types, each having its own particular role to play. They are usually in the form of three jaws borne on a stem. Certain stimuli, such as the presence of a settling larva, will cause a pedecellaria to open and then snap shut on the irritating organism. One particularly interesting variety are the glandular sort, which possess sacs of poison which can be injected into a potential predator. The most suitable sea-urchins for the aquarium are those that scavenge over rocks eating algae, barnacles, or any other organic matter. In Britain *Psammechinus* is one example. Sea-urchins that usually live in deeper waters, feeding on Laminariam, are not suitable for the aquarium.

The sea-cucumbers are worm-like echinoderms, with their

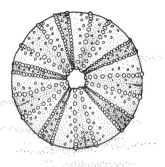

The complex skeleton, or test, of a sea-urchin. Its five-rayed symmetry is clearly visible as are the tubercles on which the spines are attached.

The sea-urchin *Psammechinus miliaris*, a browser over rocks along the shore, that is ideal for the aquarium.

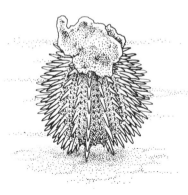

An urchin from warmer waters, *Arbacia lixula*, that has some seaweed attached to its spines.

**Fig. 49** Sea-urchins.

116

mouth at one end of their body and the anus at the other, and seem to be far removed from the penta-radial symmetry of the other members of the phylum. But in reality the radial symmetry still exists, though as they have elongated bodies and lie on their sides, there is a secondary bilateral symmetry. The five rays can still be seen as many species still have five rows of tube feet running down their bodies.

The echinoderm calcium carbonate skeleton is reduced to plates or spicules embedded in a leathery body wall.

Modified tube feet surround the mouth, and these tentacles help

**Fig. 50** The sea-cucumber *Holothuria* is found in softer substrates of the lower shore. It moves using the three rows of tube feet on its underside. The upper surface has a warty, leathery appearance. Around its mouth are a group of delicate and featherlike modified tube feet that are used in feeding. This detritivore is ideal for the aquarium, constantly passing the gravel through its digestive system.

in feeding. Often the food includes organic debris or detritus from the sea bottom, but some species extend tentacles into the water to filter feed. Strong powers of regeneration exist in sea-cucumbers – sometimes when attacked they release their guts, which soon regenerate. Most of the sea-cucumbers likely to be encountered on the shore are the detritus feeders, and are very useful aquarium inhabitants as they are constantly passing the aquarium gravel through their digestive systems, which gives them an important cleaning-up role.

## Chordata

Most of the members of this phylum possess a backbone, and these are grouped in a sub-phylum, the vertebrates. But there are also chordates that are regarded, like all the phyla mentioned earlier, as invertebrates. These chordates, though lacking a true backbone, exhibit several other chordate characteristics, such as a notochord at some stage in their life cycle. The best known of these belong to the class Ascidiacea – the ascidians or sea-squirts. Adult sea-squirts may exist as solitary individuals or in colonial forms. Their colonial forms are one of the many types of encrusting organisms that seem to cover every square centimetre of the damp, sheltered surfaces present on the shore, such as the underside of rocks and boulders.

In the adult ascidian two siphons exist, and are especially prominent in the solitary species. Beating cilia draw water into one of these, and the pharynx acts as a sieve to trap food particles. Water is then discharged through the second, exhalent, syphon. In colonial species there may be a shared exhalent syphon. All ascidians are enclosed by a protective tunic of cellulose. Though the colonial species may reproduce asexually to increase the number of individuals in the colony, all sea-squirts may also reproduce sexually. The exchange of gametes results in a free-swimming, tadpole-like larva which possesses the simple skeletal tube, the notochord, which is lost after the metamorphoses into the adult. Though the adult ascidians may seem degenerate, the

**Fig. 51** A group of solitary sea-squirts or Ascidians, *Ciona intestinalis*. They are quite common inhabitants of the lower shore and these filter feeders usually do quite well in the aquarium.

tadpole larva possess all the chordate characteristics. Besides the notochord, there is a tubular dorsal nerve cord, and also gill slits.

Colonial ascidians are often difficult to introduce into the aquarium but may, nevertheless, form colonies from larval stages. Individual species such as *Ciona* are more easy to keep. Ascidians are filter feeders so should be fed accordingly (see p. 151).

The vertebrates are a chordate sub-phylum, the members of which have a backbone composed of segmented vertebrae. Birds, reptiles and mammals all fall within this group, as do fish. Fish are in three main classes, the most primitive being the Agnatha, the lampreys and hagfish. Next come the cartilaginous fish, the Chondrichtheyes, which include the sharks, dogfish and rays. But the fish most likely to be encountered on a rocky shore fall into the third class, the Osteichthyes or bony fish.

Fish of the rocky shore may have their pelvic fin modified to form suckers, as in the case of certain gobies, which enable them to grip the rocks in buffeting waves. Some fish lack scales, and have a smooth slimy skin to facilitate movement in narrow, confined spaces. Reproduction generally involves a male fertilizing vast quantities of eggs, which hatch into pelagic larvae. Sometimes some degree of parental care is exhibited with eggs being guarded and defended from predators until they hatch. In certain blennies the male guards eggs attached to the rock, usually in a sheltered crevice. Some wrasse or sticklebacks actually construct nests out of seaweeds for their eggs.

Fish in the aquarium are usually fairly easy to cater for as most consume the standard fragments of prawn flesh, etc. Some such as pipefish require live food. Many fish, such as wrasse, are species that actively swim around and these never seem to do as well as those that remain in contact with the bottom most of the time.

**Fig. 52** The father lasher *Myoxocephalus scorpius* is a type of scorpion fish, so called because some of its spines are poisonous. It should therefore not be handled, though the stings of temperate water species are not serious. It is a very suitable fish for the aquarium, being easy to feed and small individuals will not usually bother other aquarium inhabitants. These fish spend much of their time waiting camouflaged on a rock for some suitable prey to swim past.

121

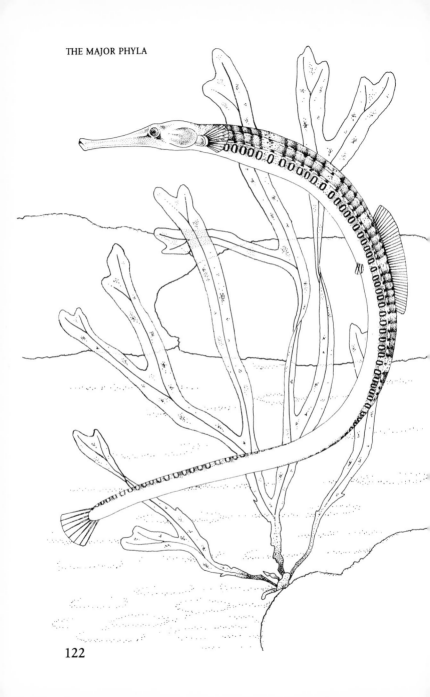

**Fig. 53** The greater pipefish *Syngnathus acus*, can grow up to 50 cm long. This fish will do well in a large aquarium and will eat about 12 small prawns each week.

Suitable fish include blennies, gobies, scorpion fish and butterfish. Always try to find small individuals for the aquarium, and also remember that two is about the right number for a small tank.

**Fig. 54** Worm pipefish *Nerophis lumbriciformis* are very small pipefish likely to be found under rocks and stones in shallow pools. They will do well in the aquarium if live food in the form of tiny crustaceans, daphnia or brine shrimps are supplied. (Overleaf)

124

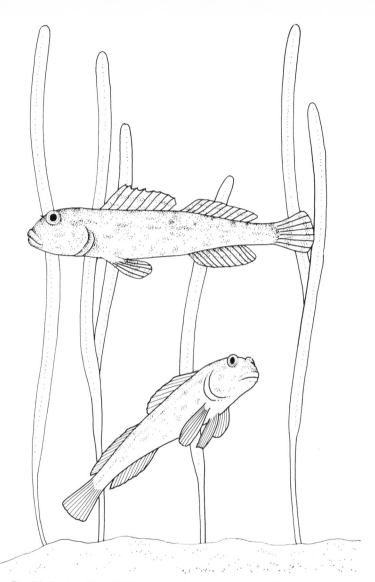

**Fig. 56** Rock gobies, *Gobius paganellus*, are common in the rock pools of Britain and Europe. Most gobies are quite suitable for the aquarium.

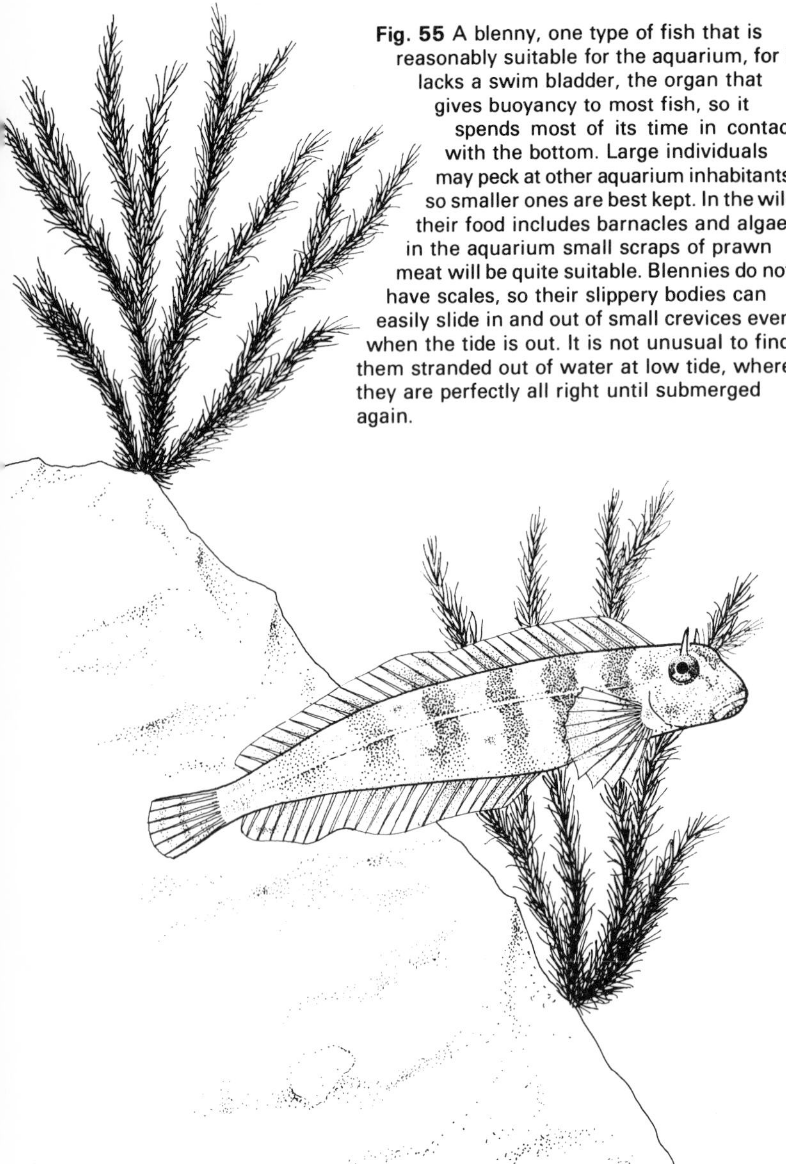

**Fig. 55** A blenny, one type of fish that is reasonably suitable for the aquarium, for it lacks a swim bladder, the organ that gives buoyancy to most fish, so it spends most of its time in contact with the bottom. Large individuals may peck at other aquarium inhabitants, so smaller ones are best kept. In the wild their food includes barnacles and algae, in the aquarium small scraps of prawn meat will be quite suitable. Blennies do not have scales, so their slippery bodies can easily slide in and out of small crevices even when the tide is out. It is not unusual to find them stranded out of water at low tide, where they are perfectly all right until submerged again.

# 6 The Seashore

It was explained in chapter 5 that rocky shores, especially in the temperate regions, provide an ideal site for gathering fascinating inhabitants for the aquarium.

Rocky shores are of infinitely variable appearance due essentially to two main factors, the type of rock and the action of the waves.

There are three main types of rock: igneous, sedimentary and metamorphic. Igneous rocks, such as granite or basalt, were originally molten magma deep within the earth, but escaped to the surface where it cooled and solidified. Sedimentary rocks are laid down over vast periods of time possibly as material suspended in ancient seas or lakes gradually sinking to the bottom, though they may also be formed on land. The loose sediments gradually became compacted by the weight of material above to form the solid rock. Limestone is a sedimentary rock formed by the compacted shells of ancient marine creatures, and sandstone is formed after other rocks are eroded and washed away as tiny fragments. Sedimentary rocks are characterized by their distinctive layers and these strata are sometimes seen to run at steep angles or even form corrugations. As they were laid down flat, this is an indication of the massive upheavals in the earth's crust that must have taken place to bend these rocks. Metamorphic rocks are rocks that were originally igneous or sedimentary but were changed from their original form by heat, pressure or chemical action. Marble is formed when molten magma is forced between layers of limestone, and slate is the result of shale being compacted under pressure.

Rocky shores, whatever the actual rock, are the result of weathering and erosion that has worn away any soft material to leave only the rocks exposed, and to varying extents all rocks are

127

constantly subject to these forces. Most erosion takes place at a rate that is too slow for us to appreciate though it is constantly occurring. The geology of a shore is worth considering because certain rocks provide ideal sites for marine life with a multitude of nooks and crannies, crevices, pools and gullies. Others may be of a flat appearance providing less secure niches for species to hide away in, or provide a substratum on which species may not be able to gain a firm grip because of the constant buffeting waves – chalks and sandstones are possible examples.

On the shore there are many different agents of weathering and erosion, and none of these work in isolation. They include rain, frost, snow, wind, evaporation, temperature changes and the boring action of certain marine animals. But the most important agent of erosion is the waves. Certain shores are open to vigorous wave action and these are termed exposed shores; in extreme cases they may be swept clean of most plants and animals so initially appear barren. But shores that are not subject to vigorous wave action, sheltered shores, are often densely colonized by seaweeds and a host of different animals that make them rich hunting grounds for those interested in marine life. But if the shore is sheltered enough to allow the accumulation of sediments, a sandy or muddy shore will result, so any rocky shore must have a certain amount of wave action. Waves are caused by the action of the wind far out at sea and spread out over the surface in the same way ripples spread over a pond. Although waves travel in definite directions the actual particles of the surface water perform only a restricted circular motion before returning to their original position. A cork or a seagull on the surface will rise and fall as a wave goes by, but remain in the same position, or at most be carried a small distance in the direction of the wave.

Waves always come in parallel to the shore, even in coves and inlets. This is due to a process called wave refraction whereby waves, even if they are travelling at right-angles to the shore, once they begin to encounter the shallower coastal water the end of the wave nearer the land is slowed down and the whole wave is bent round. Another effect on the wave as it comes into shallow water is that its top falls forward, and the wave breaks. This is because as the front of the wave reaches the shallower water first, it is slowed down first. So gradually the back will gain upon it forcing more water to the front and so the wave becomes steeper and the unsupported crest falls forward. The size of waves depends upon the speed of the wind, the length of time for which it blows and the distance over which it acts. If a fairly gentle wind has been blowing over a great distance far more powerful waves will be produced than from a much stronger wind blowing over a shorter distance.

The energy of a wave may be dissipated as the shallower water off shore causes it to break, but if there is deep water right up to the coast, off the face of a cliff for example, the waves will crash into the rock with all their force and clear signs of erosion will be visible – caves, arches or stacks. Besides the actual mass of water crashing into the rock the process of erosion may be accelerated in other ways. Sand and stones may be picked up by the waves to be hurled at the rocks, or when the wave breaks over cracks, crevices or fissures in a rock it seals in the air within them which is then compressed by the weight and force of the wave. This sudden increase in pressure, followed by an equally sudden decrease as the wave retreats, causes great stress on the rocks which eventually split and crumble.

But even on the shores most exposed to vigorous wave action there will be found many different organisms able to cope with the battering from the waves. Barnacles which are firmly cemented to the rocks, limpets clinging by adhesion, and mussels firmly anchored by their byssus threads. There are also a variety of algae; both the familiar forms and the encrusting types resembling rock. The suitability for the aquarium of these organisms varies greatly. The animals that are filter feeders, mussels and barnacles for example, will be used to regular supplies of plankton-rich water brought in by the buffeting waves. Conditions in the aquarium may be too tranquil for them, though there are mussels and barnacles from more sheltered shores which will be more suitable for the aquarium. It is not always easy to collect species on exposed shores so it is generally best to concentrate on organisms from more sheltered regions.

Besides the waves the most familiar natural phenomen of the shore is the tides, whose regular cycle – about 12 hours and 50 minutes between consecutive high or low tides – is of crucial importance in influencing where organisms live on the shore. The reason for this is that virtually all the inhabitants of the shore have evolved from marine species, used to living constantly submerged beneath the sea. Living in an area that is alternately subject to emergence (or exposure to air) at low tide, and then submergence (or being underwater) at high tide, means that these marine organisms must be able to cope with a host of new environmental constraints.

The sea offers an environment marked by consistency with no rapid changes in environmental conditions – for example temperatures change slowly and there is no danger of the environment becoming dry or even varying greatly in its salt content. Organisms living on the land, though, must be able to cope with rapidly changing conditions. Temperatures can significantly alter within a few hours – there can be drought, flood or intense radiation from the sun. The seashore is a meeting place of these two different environments and due to the tides there is a wide area whose inhabitants must be able to cope with both terrestrial and marine conditions. There are also new constraints, unique to the intertidal zone. These include the battering of the waves, and the constantly changing depth of water means that light penetration, vital for the process of photosynthesis in the algae, may at times be insufficient. Rain showers at low tide may give intertidal animals a bath in freshwater which might disrupt the salt concentration of their blood. There are also different predators to cope with, for example sea birds and waders, foxes or rats and various fish.

So there are a number of differing environmental constraints that the flora and fauna of the shore must be able to cope with. At low water there will be various physical stresses. These include drying out or dessication which can concentrate the internal fluids of an organism until normal physiological processes are stressed to a fatal level. Sun and wind can accelerate this process. Temperature fluctuations are also a problem, for though the temperature of the sea will change slowly from its summer to its winter temperature, on the shore the temperature can change by over 20°C in the course of a day, and then the incoming tide can suddenly plunge the temperature back to that of the sea, causing considerable shock to an organism.

130

Light from the sun is essential for photosynthesis in plants but the sun also emits ultra-violet radiation which, in high doses, is harmful to all living organisms. Many inhabitants of the upper regions of the shore have light-coloured shells that serve to reflect away heat and also harmful radiation – limpets and barnacles are examples. Lichens, the algae fungi symbiosis which encrust rocks right at the top of the shore, are often of very strong colours, blacks or reds, that screen out the sun's harmful rays.

The cells of many marine organisms have the concentration of their cell contents roughly equal to that of the seawater. So a sudden rain shower can change their surroundings to freshwater with the result that water will enter the cells in an attempt to equilibrate the concentration of liquids inside and outside the cell. The opposite will be true if the conditions outside the organism become more saline – as a rock pool evaporates in hot weather for example. In this case organisms will loose water from their cells. Both sorts of osmotic change cause stress.

But though many inhabitants of the intertidal zone are adapted to tolerate certain environmental stress this certainly does not mean that if 'anything goes' in the marine aquarium everything will be satisfactory. What it does mean is that if everything is done to set up and maintain the best marine system one can, then many of these organisms will be able to live in the aquarium. But even the best-maintained system will not be able to provide ideal conditions for marine life. One reason is that seawater contains such a multitude of different components, animal, vegetable and mineral, that it can never be exactly duplicated in artificial conditions. There is also light, tides and waves, all important aspects of shore life difficult to simulate at home.

When the tides are explained in the next section it will be seen their constant cycle subjects different parts of the shore to regular and predictable periods of submergence and emergence. Often bands or zonation is seen (clearly demonstrated on a harbour wall at low tide), when certain organisms, particularly seaweeds for example, or barnacles, grow only in a specific band along the shore. The upper limit of their zone is often explained by these organisms not being able to tolerate the physical stress resulting from the extra periods of emergence higher up the shore. But there is also a biological component of zonation, for example, lack of food, due possibly to a competitor, or the presence of a predator. Predation and competition (when organisms try to obtain a similar resource when there is not enough to go round) are two important factors in the distribution of a species. Competition is often for space, food or light. Many marine biologists believe that in general the upper limit of a species range is influenced by physical factors and the lower limit by biological factors. But others believe that this only applies to the upper regions of the shore and in the lower regions biological factors become all important as species are living well within the limits of their tolerance to physical stresses.

So the tides will have a profound effect on the inhabitants of the shore, but what causes them? A detailed explanation of the phenomena that cause the tides is not within the scope of this book but here is a simplified account.

As the earth and the moon spin round each other, as together they orbit the sun, two forces combine to hold them in position. Both the moon and the earth have a gravitational pull which draws them towards each other, but this force is equalled by centrifugal force which tends to hurl them apart. So they remain at a more-or-less fixed distance from each other. The liquid water masses of our planet will tend to respond far more readily to the gravitational pull of the moon, though in fact the solid earth does also experience tides, which are not easily discernible. For an explanation of the tides it is best to assume the earth is uniformly covered in water. As there are two forces holding the earth in place relative to the moon, at any point on the earth's surface the moon's gravitational pull will be in one direction and centrifugal force will pull in the opposite direction. At point X (or Y) in diagram 1, as the moon's pull (M) will be slightly greater than centrifugal force there will be a net movement of water towards point A in the diagram. This is the tidal bulge and corresponds to a high tide. But there is also a tidal bulge at point B, on the opposite side of the earth. On this side the moon's gravitational pull, due to the increased distance from the moon, is less than the centrifugal pull, which is the same all over the earth. So if point P (or Q) is considered, there is a net movement of water towards point B. This movement of water should be seen as a

*Diagram 1 a and b*

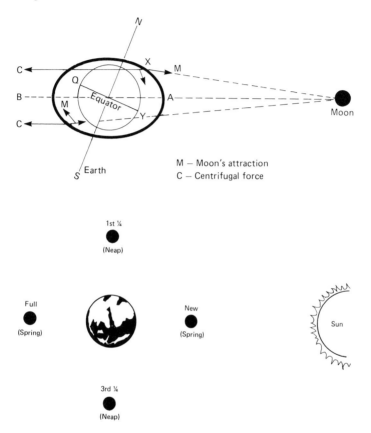

M — Moon's attraction
C — Centrifugal force

sliding round the surface of the earth, due to the sum of the two forces. As it takes just over a day for the earth to spin round so each part is directly under the moon's influence once, giving two high tides during the day. The low tides occur between the high tides, for these are at the regions from where water is lost as it is drawn to fill the bulges.

The sun also influences our tides, but due to its great distance from the earth and the moon it can only modify the moon's effect.

For example at times of new or full moon, the sun is more or less directly in line with the moon and the earth, or exactly so at times of eclipse. So the moon's effect is enhanced, and exceptionally high and low tides take place – called spring tide after the Anglo-Saxon word Springen, to rise up. But at the first and third quarters of the moon the sun and the moon are at right angles to the earth, so their pulls offset each other, giving an exceptionally small tidal range (the distance between high and low water). These tides are known as neaps.

Tidal ranges gradually oscillate over a two-week period going from spring to neap and back to spring. So each month there are two sets of spring tides which mean a larger than average area of shore will be exposed at low water – an ideal time to visit the shore. Shore life may be influenced by the fact that spring tides always occur at the same time of day in the same locality.

In this rather simplified account of the tides there has been no mention of eliptical orbits of the moon, meaning at some parts of the year it is closer to the earth than at others, thus exerting a greater gravitation pull and giving the spring tides a greater range than usual. These times, the spring and autumn equinox, are especially good periods for a visit to the shore. Of course, one must be able to find out when the spring tides occur and there are books called Tide Tables which give the height of the water above the mean water mark at all coastal locations. The highest values correspond to the spring tides though the time to visit the shore is at low water. Advice can be obtained on this from coastguards and people who own boats will also be able to help.

As a result of the tides different parts of the shore will be emerged for different periods of time. As can be seen in diagram 2, the area below point X, the lowest limits of the spring tides, will never be emerged. This is called the sub-littoral zone. Correspondingly the area above point Y, the upper limits of the spring tides, will never be submerged, but as it will be periodically splashed by spray it is called the splash zone.

Between these two regions is the littoral zone, an area which can most simply be divided into three main regions. From the mean or average level of the low water neap tides, point B down to point X

Diagram 2

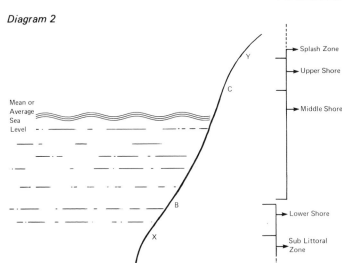

will be the lower shore. This region is emerged by low spring tides.

Above point C, the mean level of high water neap tides, up to point Y, is the upper shore, an area only submerged by high spring tides. Between these regions is the middle shore, regularly submerged and emerged.

## COLLECTING FROM THE SHORE

A collecting expedition to the shore can be a fascinating day out. First locate a good shore, a rocky shore will be best, and remember to find out at what time low tide is – spring tides will be especially good periods. Equipment to be taken must include plastic bags plus a variety of plastic containers to use on the shore, also containers that can be sealed up in which to transport things back home. Orange juice or icecream containers are particularly suitable but soap or bleach containers are not, however well they may have been rinsed as they are toxic substances. A large insulated container such as a large picnic hamper is useful as well. Some can actually be used as small portable aquaria kept in the back of the car, but even if they are not used for this purpose, as they may be too heavy to handle or possibly leak, they are still very useful in providing insulation for the other containers, to prevent organisms overheating on the journey back. Other useful equipment includes a hammer and chisel to use in carefully chipping off bits of rock, and also nets of varying sizes for swishing about in pools and in the sea itself. Spades are useful in revealing certain inhabitants of sandy or muddy shores.

When arriving at the shore it is best to go as far down the shore as possible for there will be a greater variety of species lower down the shore. Rocks and stones, without potentially harmful veins of metal running through them, will be important in the newly set up tank. Try to find ones with plenty of life growing on them, including red and green algae. Larger rocks, which may not be able to be transported home submerged, will be quite all right wrapped in seaweed to keep them damp and enclosed in a strong plastic bag.

Some specimens will be found under stones and boulders, some will be attached to weeds or rocks. Certain organisms like anemones can be detached by gently inserting a finger nail between their basal disc and the rock to prise them loose. Some organisms may be firmly insinuated in a crevice so will have to be carefully exposed with a hammer and chisel. Never risk damaging a species if it cannot be got at. This is just one of the many ecological considerations that should be remembered. Don't collect species that are rare or that occur in low numbers, only those that exist in reasonable populations, and if you turn over a rock to see what is lurking underneath don't leave it upside down but return it to its original position. Finally, be careful with the hammer and chisel to ensure only minimum damage to the environment is caused. (Mind your eyes, too, in case a chip of rock flies up.) A far more likely personal injury will be caused by slipping on the lush seaweeds, so some form of footwear that will help in gripping should be worn. Also the odd plastic dressing will be useful in case cuts occur.

When collecting on the shore remember rock pools, particularly on the lower regions of the shore, which are fruitful hunting grounds. Here there are organisms used to continual submergence and in an environment though superficially like a natural aquarium, in fact subject to possible wild fluctuations in pH, temperature and all the other potential stresses of intertidal life. The coralline algae, so common in rock pools in the temperate region don't always do well in aquaria, but it's always worth trying a tiny clump – for your aquarium may offer just the right conditions for them to grow.

Remember also not to over-collect. This applies especially to anemones and fish. Try if possible to plan out the tank you want to have. You may not be able to organize it all in one visit, or even in a season, but this is far better than a totally unbalanced system with an abundance of some creatures and an obvious lack of others.

If an extended trip to the shore is planned specimens can be gathered over many days if there is a temporary aquarium set up. A polystyrene box is especially good but a large plastic container will also do. Remember to aerate this constantly with an air pump and airstone, and change most of the water at least once a day.

When all the collecting is over it will be important to get the organisms back home quickly – within half a day if possible. If natural seawater is also being collected for the tank then even a few hours may be too long.

Here again the insulated polystyrene box is useful, especially if it has a secure lid that will prevent water spilling into the car. Other containers, too, can be used, but these are best only half filled so the water will be aerated. Artificial aeration for the journey home will not be necessary if specimens are not overcrowded.

Some creatures must not be transported in the same container as others – anemones are a classic example, for though an animal such as a small fish or crab may be quite capable of avoiding an anemone in normal circumstances, being thrown around together in the back of a car may result in the anemone stinging and possibly eating the other unfortunate creature.

Once you get back home it is not possible to immediately dump everything into the tank. Of course, rocks and weeds might as well go straight in but more delicate organisms should be gradually acclimatized. This is best done by keeping them in a plastic bag with their original seawater. This bag is immersed in the tank so the temperatures can equilibrate. Then carefully allow the two waters to gradually mix, so after about half an hour the bag contents, animal and water, can be poured into the tank.

A footnote to this section on collecting involves the use of snorkelling or even scuba diving to greatly increase the variety of specimens one can keep in the aquarium. Shallow water contains many organisms not found between the tides, that are ideal for the aquarium. But remember that diving, especially, can be dangerous so learn this by joining a proper diving club.

## WARM WATER SYSTEMS

This book would not be complete without mention of species from warmer or even tropical waters.

The difficulties of artificially cooling a home aquarium have already been gone into (pp. 38–41). But keeping a tank at a Mediterranean temperature of around 20°C or a tropical temperature of around 25°C is quite simple using the combined heater and thermostat units, housed in a large test tube, which are comparatively cheap.

Warm water tanks, keeping organisms from sunnier climes, will benefit from brighter lights turned on for at least 12 hours a day. An additional bright spot light is also very useful. There are some warm water species of algae – *Caulerpa* is one – that will grow well and benefit from the light, for they do naturally receive plenty of light in their clearer waters.

Apart from these factors the basic principles are the same for all marine systems.

The roles of the different organisms in warm water communities are in many ways similar in all marine waters. There will be herbivores, carnivores, filter feeders and detrivores.

One big difference between tropical and temperate waters is in the type of algae they support. The huge quantities of large algae, such as wracks and laminarians, growing in cooler waters are not present in the tropics. Instead many of the algae are either stone-like calcareous species or single cells symbiotically associated with many species of corals, and also anemones and clams. Corals feed by filter feeding as well, but do need bright light especially if they

**Fig. 57** Seahorses are generally associated with warmer waters. These are close relatives of the pipefish. The male broods the young in a small pouch after the female has laid the eggs there. Seahorses need live food in the aquarium.

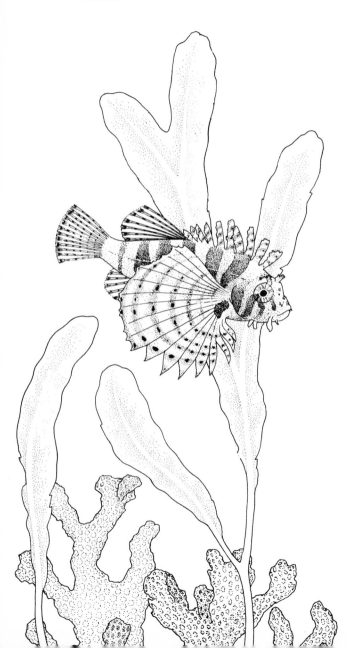

contain these symbiotic algae. It seems by living inside coral tissue these algae gain protection and can utilize waste products from the coral's metabolism. The coral gain by having these waste products taken up by the algae and then benefiting from the products of the algae's photosynthesis.

Coral reefs, in common with tropical rain forests, support a number and diversity of species unequalled in other ecosystems. As a result of this there have evolved many highly specialized feeders, many symbiotic relationships and a multitude of poisonous animals. This could well be due to the fact that in the tropics there is a stable and constant condition, often unchanged for millions of years, so there has been time for specialists to evolve. In temperate waters the regular seasonal changes with associated fluctuations in environmental conditions such as temperature, has resulted in fewer species, and species that are often less specialized – there are many 'generalists' who can eat a variety of foods, according to what is available at the time, and tolerate fluctuating conditions.

One fascinating aspect of life in tropical waters involves mimicry and the cleaning symbiosis. Many different types of mimicry exist, and one of these is when a species that is for some reason inedible to a particular predator is imitated by another species that would otherwise be an acceptable prey.

The result is that the predator may be deceived into thinking that the edible creature, termed the mimic, is of the same species as the inedible one, termed the model. It will therefore harm neither.

Another type of mimicry is termed *aggressive*. Here the predator mimics a non-predator species. In doing so it may be able to deceive its prey into believing it is harmless and so get close enough to attack.

There is also the phenomenon which involves poisonous or unpalatable species adopting a similar colour scheme. Combinations of black, white and yellow are often used to warn other species, as in the case of the lion fish and certain nudibranchs.

**Fig. 58** A lion fish, a tropical relative of the temperate water scorpion fish, that is more poisonous. It is a remarkably beautiful fish that generally needs live food in order to survive in the aquarium.

One fascinating example of mimicry occurs in the Red Sea. It involves the cleaner wrasse *Labroides dimidiatus*. The cleaner wrasse is one of 42 species of fish known to act as cleaners in the tropics – removing skin parasites, and diseased and damaged skin from larger fish. Some crustaceans perform a similar role (usually brightly coloured shrimps with conspicuous waving antennae).

Cleaners live in a specific territory on the coral reef, known as a cleaning station, and larger fish pass through to be cleaned. Full-time cleaners – the cleaner wrasse included – exist only by their cleaning actions. Other part-time, or semi-professional cleaners supplement their diets with more conventional foods such as plankton.

When a large fish such as a grouper arrives at a cleaning station, it will queue up if the cleaner is busy. When it is actually being cleaned it becomes particularly docile, even allowing the cleaner to enter its mouth and gills.

The cleaner wrasse *Labroides* uses conspicuous signals to inform a potential predator that it is a cleaner which should not be harmed. These include a peculiar swimming motion involving beating the pectoral fins like the wings of a butterfly, and a conspicuous colour scheme of light and dark stripes.

*Labroides*, however, is imitated in both swimming motion and colour by the sabre-tooth blenny *Aspidontus taeniatus*. The mimic will lure a fish that is intending to be cleaned until it becomes docile enough for it to bite off a bit of its fin! Even though the hurt fish may turn angrily the blenny's mimicry ensures that it is not attacked.

It is usually younger, inexperienced fish that fall victim to *Aspidontus*'s act. Older fish gradually learn to distinguish the cleaner from its mimic, and to ensure that the cleaning operation starts at its head. When the blenny ignores this region in an attempt to get at the fins the 'customer' will realize the deception.

The cleaning symbiosis though is not unique to the tropics. In

**Fig. 59** This is a tropical holothorian or sea-cucumber. It's tube feet are visible, its feeding apparatus is partially withdrawn. When fully extended it forms a dense net used to filter feed.

temperate waters pipefish will clean the John Dory, and cork wing wrasse will clean sea-bream, which will line up, waiting their turn. Grey mullet have also been observed cleaning nurse hounds.

One of the best known symbiotic associations of tropical waters involves the clown fish, most of which belong to the genus *Amphiprion*, which live amongst the tentacles of sea anemones. Except for a brief larval period clown fish will not survive for long if separated from their host anemone.

It seems that the clown fish/sea anemone symbiosis is mutualistic, meaning that both partners benefit – the fish gain protection from their predators by the anemone's stinging tentacles, and may also be less susceptible to parasites. They may also gain food from the anemone. The anemone gains as the clown fish will chase away fish that feed on anemones, such as butterfly fish and the clown fish will also clean the anemone, removing dead or decaying tissue. The clown fish are immune to the anemone's stinging cells, but this immunity has to be built up over a period of a few hours. A clown fish that has not been in contact with an anemone for a time will be stung if it swims directly back into the tentacles.

It is believed that in this acclimitization period the clown fish alters the layer of mucus that covers its body so that the anemone's stinging cells will not be stimulated when they make contact with the fish.

Clown fish have a special problem in reproduction and the successful maintenance of their population because their host anemones are not predictably distributed. After hatching, the larval clown fish swim freely in plankton, and this is how the species is distributed. Once they find an anemone, however, they are reluctant to move, due to their vulnerability to predation.

If clown fish were orthodox and produced offspring in a 1:1 sex ratio (ie 50% males and 50% females), there would be a possibility that two clown fish arriving at an anemone would be of the same sex. If both were males or both females, breeding could not take

**Fig. 60** The banded coral shrimps *Stenopus*, whose conspicuous appearance ensures it is recognized as a 'cleaner'. These shrimps are one of the many marine creatures that derive some proportion of their dietary needs by picking dead tissue and parasites from other organisms, usually larger fish.

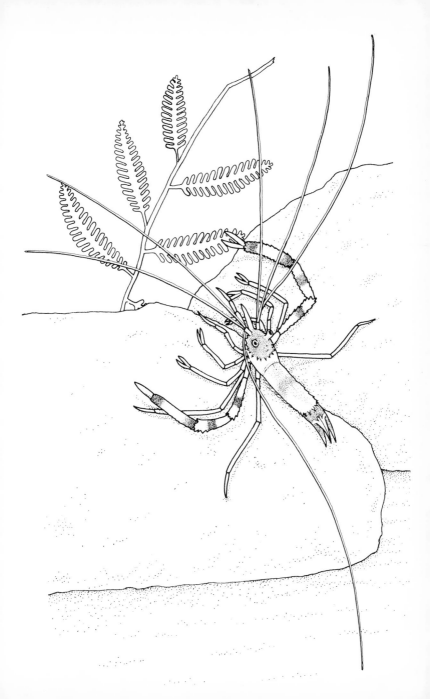

**Fig. 61** A tropical marine aquarium may look like this. The set up includes, from left to right:
a soft coral and a fan worm;
organ pipe coral and a clam;
anemones and another soft coral;
two false corals and an algae;
a cleaner shrimp and a sea-cucumber.
In the large anemone (Radianthus) there is a clown fish and an anemone shrimp and at the back there is a Picasso trigger fish.

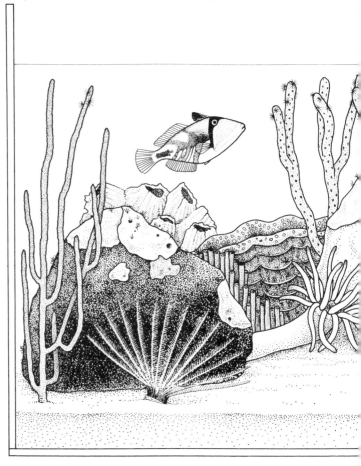

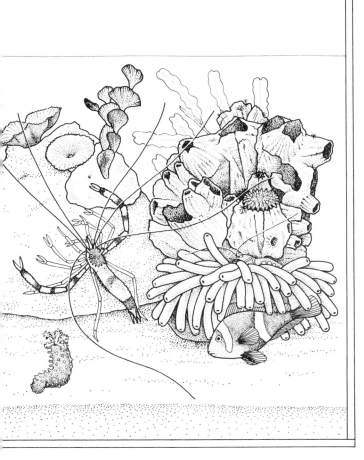

place and, if these individuals were forced to change anemones, energy and life would be wasted.

The solution to this problem is a form of sequential hermaphroditism, where an individual first functions as one sex, then as the other. Many types of fish undergo sex changes, for example the wrasses (*Labridae*). In the case of wrasses, the rationale seems to be that an area of reef can support only a certain number of individuals. For example, if it supported six individuals, one male fertilizing five females will result in many more offspring being produced than if there were three females being fertilized by three males. The male is dominant over the females and, if he should disappear, the dominant female below him in the hierarchy becomes the male. This is known as protogynous hermaphroditism but, in the clown fish's case, the process is reversed and proteandric hermaphroditism occurs where individuals function first as males and then as females.

In the Red Sea a group of the clown fish, *Amphiprion akallopisas*, form a 'pecking order'. The most aggressive fish becomes the dominant female and by aggressive dominance ensures that no other fish become female and that younger fish do not develop sexually. The number two in the pecking order is a male fish – the female's mate – whose aggressive dominance prevents all its subordinates from spawning. The lower ranking males are psychosociologically castrated, and their gonads do not develop fully. It was shown that, if the dominant female was removed, every member of the hierarchy moved up one rung. So the dominant male, previously the female's mate, became the dominant female after a few weeks. The second most dominant male in the previous hierarchy now moved up to be the dominant male and so be the mate of the newly developed female. The rest of the group remained subordinate.

It has not been proved that all clown fish follow this exact pattern of sexual development though and there are differences between the species. However, all clown fish, through highly specialized adaptations, such as socially controlled sex changes and immunity to stinging, have learnt to exploit anemones and so obtain a secure niche in a potentially hostile environment.

This immunity to the anemone's stinging cells may be shared by tropical crabs and prawns, which also live associated with the anemone. In temperate waters, too, certain spider crabs live sheltered beneath the tentacles of some species of anemone.

# 7 Maintenance

## FEEDING
In the intertidal zone the organisms, from the point of view of the marine aquarist, can be broken down into six major feeding strategies. Some can easily be catered for, but some are more difficult.

### The herbivores
These are animals that eat plant matter, and in the marine aquarium it generally means the scraping off of the micro-algae that grows on all the surfaces of the tank. The mouth of such creatures is usually adapted to rasping away at the thin layer of algae and examples include snails, such as top shells *Gibula* or limpets, *Patella*, or sea-urchins such as *Psammechinus*. Chitons and periwinkles are also within this category.

In a reasonably well-lit aquarium a good growth of micro-algae (as opposed to the larger fronds of the macro-algae) will soon occur. For a small tank with a good growth of micro-algae two or three herbivores are usually quite enough for the limited food supply.

On rocky shores many species of seaweed, such as kelps and laminarians, once they have reached a certain size, are unpalatable to most herbivores. Yet the stage in which they settle, the sporeling, is readily consumed, and intertidal herbivores have a profound effect in keeping many areas completely clear of seaweeds by never allowing their sporelings to develop.

### The carnivores
This group includes a host of intertidal organisms that includes anemones, many worms, molluscs such as whelks, crabs, prawns,

and many fish species. Though in their natural state they all feed on very different things, their needs in the aquarium can be simply catered for.

They will all relish the flesh of the pink boiled prawns obtainable at most fishmongers. It is essential that the food is fresh, and this applies to any matter supplied to the aquarium creatures. These prawns are best kept in the deep freeze and at feeding times one can be taken out and a small piece broken off. Then a tiny fragment of the meat can be given for each animal. For fish such as blennies it is quite sufficient to drop the food near them, they will soon find it. For anemones it is important to ensure the food is directed to the animals' tentacles and a glass or wooden rod with a tapering, but blunt, end is useful for this. It is best to put one's hand in the tank as infrequently as possible.

Alternatives to fresh boiled prawn include scraps of the flesh of any fresh fish. The flesh of mussels is also very useful and readily taken. Finally, your aquarist's shop will sell frozen sterilized foods that are very handy, for they can be kept in the deep freeze at home. The secret of feeding is little and often, say about twice a week – overfeeding is very bad for the aquarium. Also, try to occasionally vary the food offered. Occasionally the addition of live food (see pp. 153–4), will also be appreciated.

### Detritivores

These are animals that generally live in and on the gravel at the bottom of the tank. Their food includes the leftovers and waste of the other animals in the tank, especially the carnivores, but they will also eat scraps of prawn flesh and other foods. They are therefore very useful and important inhabitants, being the cleaners of the tank.

This group includes certain whelks, sea-cucumbers, brittle stars and many species of worm. Many other aquarium inhabitants will also do some cleaning up, hermit crabs and prawns are examples, for many intertidal organisms are opportunists – finding food wherever they can.

### Filter feeders

These are a group of animals that take advantage of the huge food resources of the plankton. Planktonic life includes single-celled plants, small animals that eat these plants, and also the mobile larval stages of many marine creatures. Seawater also contains vast quantities of bacteria and, in temperate regions, many tiny fragments which have been broken off seaweeds. These, too, are important foods for filter feeders, especially as fragments of seaweeds are rapidly colonized by bacteria, which make them even more nutritious.

Filter feeders are such creatures as the beautiful fan-worms, barnacles, mussels as well as a host of the small encrusting organisms that are found on rocks and weed. These include sponges, small anemones and bryozoa.

The sea's plankton provides a source of food that may be subject to seasonal fluctuations. It is not always easy to keep filter feeders; one of the best ways, if you live by the sea and can ensure unpolluted water, is to regularly change a few pints of water. This way new planktonic life will be introduced.

For those living further from the sea there are alternatives to natural plankton. First, make your own sea-food cocktail. Put mussel flesh, prawns or any fresh fish meat plus vegetable matter such as the sea lettuce *Ulva*, boiled spinach, or raw garden lettuce, in the liquidiser or use a mortar and pestle to make a nutrient-rich liquid. This must then be kept in the deep freeze and every few days a bit can be chipped off and defrosted in the tank so no goodness escapes. A visit to the seashore can supply many of the ingredients – use what you can find. Remember that any food must be fresh, and deep freezers help greatly in storage. You may also purchase proprietry brands of food for filter feeders. Some deep-frozen brands are sterilized by gamma-radiation and contain no chemical preservatives – these are quite good.

A final solution is in the most versatile aquarium food – the fishmongers' boiled prawn. The head region when squeezed in the water will release a thick cloudy liquid rich in nutrients which provides food for filter feeders.

The marine aquarium like the sea supports vast quantities of bacteria – most live in the filter bed, but they also colonize every available surface, as well as living freely in the water. As these invisible bacteria are consumed by many filter feeders, they may well be feeding when there is no food immediately apparent, and this might be why certain filter feeders will do well in the aquarium.

It must be remembered that as for all organisms only a certain number of filter feeders can be kept in the tank. They will all compete for food and as opposed to some organisms that can clearly be seen to consume a scrap of prawn flesh, one can never be sure how much a filter feeder is actually getting. Some filter feeders may do well in the aquarium, yet others will slowly die. It may be that a species will only feed on the plankton from natural seawater, or needs to detect the presence of a specific food substance before it begins to feed. Others only feed at a rate proportional to the amount of food present. Under natural conditions this would mean they would save energy until more food became available again, but in the aquarium it may mean they will gradually starve unless they receive enough of the right sort of food.

Certain filter feeders may require strong currents to feed, or will not feed if the chemical balance of the water is not quite right for them.

Here again is an aspect of marine aquarium keeping to which no hard and fast rules apply – your aquarium might offer just the right conditions in which a species will thrive though it will not live in another apparently similar tank.

## Live food

Certain carnivores will not eat fragments of flesh, but will only take small swimming organisms such as small prawns or shrimps. Regular water changes, as suggested for filter feeders, may be sufficient for some of these creatures, but some will require the addition of live food.

These include the fifteen-spined stickleback or the greater pipe-fish, both of which are especially beautiful and fascinating and worth the extra trouble, but they need bigger tanks – 3 to 4 foot long.

Many local aquarist shops now sell live food in the form of brine shrimps and sometimes the slightly larger mysis shrimps. These will be readily taken, but if a regular supply is not easily available an alternative is to culture brine shrimp at home. Their eggs can be bought and should be placed in a plastic or glass vessel that contains

153

seawater. It should be aerated and you may be able to put an extra gang valve in your air tubing from the pump and run air off that, or buy a cheap pump (it is good to have a spare one anyway). In this set up, an air store is very useful.

If the water is heated to about 24°C the shrimps will hatch sooner, and small aquarium heaters can be bought fairly cheaply. After a few days the eggs will hatch and a small net can be used to scoop out the brine shrimp. They may, of course, be allowed to grow. It is quite possible to get a self-perpetuating colony, but remember to feed these filter feeders and periodically change the water in their container.

There are other sources of live food. Many aquarist shops stock tiny common prawns. These organisms are fascinating marine aquarium inhabitants in their own right but if species like the greater pipefish are kept they will need them as a food, as the brine shrimp are too small to satisfy them.

Another useful live food often stocked in aquarium shops is the common water flea *Daphnia*. These freshwater organisms can also be gathered from ponds or cultured in water butts. They will live for a brief period in the marine tank where smaller species of pipefish as well as many other organisms will relish them. For even if certain aquarium inhabitants, such as certain fish, will live happily on scraps of prawn or mussel flesh an occasional change of diet, to include live food, is very beneficial. Certain filter feeders such as small anemones or mussels will also take *Daphnia*.

Some marine aquaria support populations of small crustaceans, often gammarids or copepods. These could have been introduced with natural seawater or brought in with some rocks. The fact that these organisms are maintaining their population in the tank is good news. Not only are they a food source for other aquarium inhabitants but the fact that they are breeding in the tank is an indication the aquarium is being well maintained.

## Specialist feeders

There are some intertidal organisms that only eat very specific food items. Obviously if these food items are readily obtainable they can be kept, but for most people these organisms are best left alone.

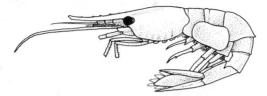

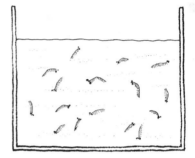

**Fig. 62** Food for the aquarium. At the top the useful boiled prawn. Underneath a small container of brine shrimps – useful live food. There are also the proprietory brands of aquarium food.

155

One example of specialist feeders is the different species of sea-slugs that can be found on the rocky shores, especially during the summer.

The sea-lemon *Archidoris pseudoargus* eats only sponges. The common grey sea-slug *Aeolidia papillosa* eats usually snakelocks or beadlet anemones. Sea-slugs are often extremely delicate and beautiful animals. But it is not right to gather them unless they can be properly looked after.

There are many species of sea-slugs in Britain and these are described in *British Opisthobranch Molluscs* by T.E. Thompson and G.M. Brown (see Further Reading, p. 170). One clue to their food is to observe where they are found – it is often close to or even on their food source. In many cases they are camouflaged to resemble their food as well. But animals such as these are best left to the more experienced aquarist.

So to sum up this section on feeding, freshness and variety are very important. Try giving live food to all organisms, even those that will take other forms of food, and experiment occasionally. For example a fresh lettuce leaf dropped in the tank may be enjoyed by a variety of organisms. Finally, don't ignore the dry flaked foods available for marine aquarists, these too might be appreciated occasionally.

## WATER CHANGES

Regularly changing a small quantity of the water in the aquarium – any amount around $\frac{1}{2}$ to 1 gallon about every two months – is one of the most important things to do in the successful running of an aquarium.

There are a variety of reasons for this. Earlier on (pp. 23–4) reference was made to pH and buffers, saying that it was important that the aquarium was always at the right degree of alkalinity, or more scientifically, at a pH of about 8.3. A regular change of seawater will help maintain this correct pH level.

Another benefit of water changes is that in seawater there is a variety of trace elements, substances which, though present in very small amounts, are essential for living plants and animals. In an aquarium, as organisms live and grow they may use up some of these trace elements so that other things may be disadvantaged to some degree. By periodically changing the water the essential trace elements are replaced.

## How to do it

When the water is changed the first thing to do is to remove some of the old water. The best way to do this is to use the principle of the syphon. A length of plastic air pipe is filled with water so there is no air in the pipe at all. Then with one end constantly in the aquarium water, the other end, while being sealed using a finger, is taken out and held at a level lower than that of the end that is in the tank.

When the finger is taken away water will flow out, and is best caught in a container of known volume so approximately the same amount of new water can be returned. It is possible to stir the gravel up a little at this time so some of the detritus (the harmless end product of the bacterial breakdown of the animal's waste products) can be sucked out with the seawater. If stirring up the gravel makes the aquarium water very cloudy it is a good indication there is too much detritus in the tank and a clean-out is needed.

When the old water is removed gently pour in the new seawater. It may be that the old water has a slight yellowish hue. This is less likely if the charcoal filter mentioned earlier is used, and though it is not too serious it is better that the water be as clear as possible and the regular water changes help greatly in this.

It may be asked whether the seawater used for these partial water changes should be natural seawater or artificial. Exactly the same applies as described in chapter 1 – both are acceptable. From the convenience point of view as well as avoiding pollution problems artificial seawater stored in a clean plastic dustbin is often best. A small amount of water is then taken out for the water changes. It is advantageous to keep a lid on the bin to stop dust entering and to have a stream of bubbles constantly aerating the water. Either use an air pipe from your main pump if it is powerful enough, or use another small cheap pump.

If you feel you have an unpolluted source of seawater then it has one distinct advantage if it can be introduced into the aquarium within a few hours of being collected. Many marine creatures have a stage in their life cycles – usually the first few days of their lives

157

– when they exist on tiny larvae. Their presence in seawater, especially in the spring and summer in the temperate zones, makes natural seawater interesting; for even though it is very hard even to see these tiny creatures, there is often a chance that some will settle and grow into their adult form in the aquarium. Others may serve as a useful food source for other aquarium inhabitants – especially the filter feeders. Besides larvae there may also be beneficial single-celled algae, tiny crustaceans and vast quantities of bacteria that are also useful.

If quantities of natural seawater are available it can also be kept in the plastic dustbin as long as it is constantly aerated. Of course, most of the planktonic organisms will die but the seawater will be perfectly satisfactory for the tank. In fact if natural seawater is gathered and it cannot be introduced into the tank within a few hours, it is best left aerating for a few days. This is because after a few hours in transit the planktonic organisms will start to die off, and soon the seawater will be a foul soup of dead organisms. But by steadily aerating this water for a few days it will stabilize and be perfectly suitable for water changes.

A final point in water changing is to ensure that the water being added to the tank is of the same concentration as that in the tank – so measure both with the hydrometer. The reason for this is that the concentration of the body fluids of many of the aquarium inhabitants will be the same as that of the surrounding water. If a lot of water is added that is of a different concentration to that of the tank it may put a stress on some of the creatures as they adapt to the new conditions.

## OTHER MAINTENANCE

Once the aquarium has been set up and is running in a satisfactory fashion, besides feeding and the regular partial water changes there is very little that will need doing.

Air tubing may collect a gradual build-up of salt right at the end, and this restricts the air flow. This deposit builds up over a period of months and is easily removed by taking out the tubing and squeezing the end so the salt deposit is broken up. Air tubing may become hard and inflexible after a long period of immersion in the water, but this does not affect its efficiency.

It is possible, though not really necessary, to monitor changes in the pH and also the build-up and breakdown of the waste products formed in the aquarium, the nitrate and nitrite balance. Test kits can be purchased for this purpose. The pH of a tank will quite naturally vary throughout the course of the day. It was explained in the secretion on pH (p. 23–4), how the activities of the organisms in the aquarium may affect this slightly but in a balanced aquarium, the water circulation will prevent any problems occurring.

Over a period of time the pH of a tank may gradually decrease for the buffering qualities of the gravel may become less efficient, but the partial water changes will ensure it remains stable. So in the established aquarium testing for pH will be an academic exercise and not worthwhile.

It is possible to purchase chemical buffers that will maintain a stable pH, though if it is ever found that the pH is not right a partial water change puts things right, rather than putting chemicals in the tank. The other test mentioned – nitrate and nitrite – will also be unnecessary in an established tank. As was explained these factors may be a problem at first but if the aquarium is set up step by step with the inhabitants being gradually introduced no problem should occur.

## Salinity

So pH and nitrate/nitrite tests are not necessary but one test is useful and that is periodically ensuring that the water of the tank has not become too saline. As with the mixing of artificial seawater, this is easily measured with an hydrometer and the correct value is 1.024. It could well be some of the water has evaporated from the tank so the water left will become more concentrated, for the salt will not evaporate out. The simple solution is to top up with some fresh water. The reverse situation, where the water in the tank is too dilute, cannot reasonably occur. It must be remembered that the specific gravity of seawater will change slightly according to its temperature. For example at 20°C (68°F) the SG = 1.024 but at 16°C (51°F) SG = 1.025. There is a table at the back of all these specific gravity, temperature ratios (p. 169).

159

## Temperature

Keep an eye on the temperature but as was explained earlier (pp. 38–41), it's very difficult to cool tank water.

## A COMPLETE CLEAN-OUT

If the aquarium is set up with the standard undergravel filter and airpump system, in about a year, depending on the amount of animals being kept in the tank, detritus, the harmless end product of the bacterial breakdown of the waste products of the animals, will need to be removed. It is unsightly, may clog up the filter or be stirred up to cloud the water. So a complete clean-out of a tank will have to be made.

First, unplug the lights and the pump and then all the animals, plants and rocks will have to be taken out of the tank and immediately immersed in water that has just been taken out of the aquarium. You may need extra clean (i.e. not soapy, oily or dirty) buckets or bowls. Plastic, glass or earthenware ones will do, as it is only for an hour or two. It is a good idea to combine this major annual clean-out with an overdue partial water change, so have a good quantity of natural or artificial seawater ready.

When the animals, rocks, etc. have been placed in the bowls, immersed in the aquarium water, the rest of the water is no longer needed and can be thrown away. Make sure though you do not throw away more old seawater than you have new water to replace it with. When the aquarium is empty, except for the gravel (and the UG filter of course), start scooping out the gravel. Little by little rinse it out under the cold tap by putting some gravel in the bottom of a clean plastic bucket, adding some water and swilling it around. When the water is a dirty brown colour pour away the water, and place the gravel in a separate container. Repeat this process until all the gravel is removed from the tank, then remove the UG filter or filters. Rinse these out and, using a clean, absorbent cloth or sponge, remove any gunge left at the bottom of the aquarium. Then return the UG filter(s) and then the cleaned gravel.

Now pour back some of the original seawater and return the animals and rocks. Then top up with fresh natural or artificial seawater. Quickly, get the pump going again, turn on the lights and breathe a sigh of relief. If the water is a bit cloudy it will soon clear and the inhabitants soon settle down again.

There are situations when the glass itself has fascinating growth of organisms on it. These may be a particular seaweed or colonial animals such as bryozoa, sea-squirts or sponges. In this case a complete water change leaving these creatures high and dry for an hour or two could be fatal. One possible solution is to ensure these creatures remain damp throughout the exercise by covering them with cotton-wool or tissues soaked in seawater or simply by splashing them every now and then with seawater. For if they remain wet they will probably survive.

## PITFALLS AND COMMON MISTAKES

Many of the potential problems of the marine aquarium will, I hope, have been dealt with in this book, but it might be useful to highlight some of the common mistakes.

The first is overfeeding. A well set-up aquarium will have a small population of herbivores, carnivores and detritivores whose activities will complement each other. If too much food is given it will have to be broken down by the bacteria and so might put a strain on the filtration process of the tank, and just promote a build up of detritus. So remember small amounts of food about twice a week.

The second point is overcrowding. An ideal aquarium set-up has a balance of different organisms, and under no conditions is a crowded tank more interesting or in any way preferable to a sparsely populated one. In a 2-foot tank a few small fish, two or three small anemones plus some other carnivores, detritivores and herbivores will be quite enough. There will, of course, be many rocks with their associated encrusting organism. Larger aquaria can house more organisms, but the principle of a balance of species still applies.

Place no chemicals or metals in the water, and try to keep noxious chemicals out of the room in which the aquarium is. These include insecticides, tobacco smoke and household cleaning fluids that contain ammonia.

Look out for rocks that are found at the shore which may have veins of metal in them that could harm the aquarium inhabitants.

Though it has been suggested that red and green algae are worth trying, if they are seen to be rotting they must be immediately removed from the tank.

As a general rule always remember that many highly successful and experienced marine aquarists have the most simple and basic set-ups. It is their knowledge and experience, probably starting off with a few of the easier-to-keep species, and learning from them, that paved the way to their success. Do not be misled, or even put off, by those who say that you must have expensive or complicated gadgets or special chemical additives in order to succeed.

It might also be worth adding at this point that at various sections in this book there has been a reference to biological breakdown, the distressing occurrence when an avalanche effect of a build-up of waste products combines with detrimental changes in pH and oxygen levels in the tank. But let it be stressed that this will not occur in a tank that is properly maintained with no overcrowding. If the filtration system was to stop working for many hours during the night, in a power cut for example, the aquarium could have problems as the water circulation ceased, but this is very unlikely. And it is acceptable to stop the circulation temporarily for maintenance, feeding or water changes, if the tank is not in darkness at the time. So do not be put off by a phenomenon unknown to careful marine aquarists.

Another point worth mentioning here is disease. One can often find references to disease in aquarium literature, particularly those catering for tropical systems, and they usually refer to problems with fish, fungal or bacterial infections for example. In this book there has been a strong emphasis on keeping just a few fish living as part of a balanced community with other organisms. In such systems I have never encountered disease and believe it is yet another manifestation of overpopulation or poor maintenance. Of course some organisms will die, possibly due to temperature stress or the lack of the right sort of food, but this does not happen often in aquaria that are carefully set up and looked after.

## BREEDING MARINE AQUARIUM ORGANISMS

There is no greater testimony to a successfully maintained marine aquarium than when certain organisms start to breed. It is, though, an unusual occurrence, for either fish or invertebrates to produce larvae that will survive into adulthood in the tank, and usually the best one can hope for is when a pair of organisms mate and fertile eggs are produced. The resulting larvae will usually die due to unfavourable conditions, insufficient food of the right type, or they may be eaten by other organisms.

Yet there are aquarists who do breed marine organisms and with their experience plus new developments in aquarium technology it is hoped that one day soon the breeding and rearing of marine organisms will be as common as it is in freshwater systems. This will be a major step forward, because not only will it reduce the slight stress on the environment caused by collecting, but also organisms will be able to be returned to the sea to help repopulate and recolonize polluted or damaged environments.

In some of the cases where marine organisms do breed it is more by chance than design, though an understanding of the life cycles of the marine organisms certainly helps. So does trying to keep organisms in pairs rather than as odd individuals. Some organisms like fish are of separate sex so a male and female must be selected. This also applies to certain invertebrates, although some are hermaphrodites.

The life cycle of many marine creatures involves a free-swimming larval stage between egg and adult. This is crucial in the distribution of species, especially those that are sessile, such as barnacles or sponges. The length of most larvae of seashore organisms is measured in a fraction of a millimetre, or at best millimetres, when they are first released. After a period of growth and development as free-living planktonic organisms the larvae try to seek a suitable area to spend their adult lives, which is often in a fairly small territory, and the larvae of sessile species, once they metamorphose into the adult form, will not be able to change their position.

Larvae form a large part of the diet of many filter feeders and filter feeders living in an aquarium have been known to eat not only the larvae of other organisms but even their own offspring. Larvae often exhibit instinctive behaviour patterns, for example by swimming towards light when first released, thus avoiding bottom-dwelling filter feeders.

Whilst living in the open sea the larvae will feed on other planktonic organisms which may be single-celled algae, tiny crustaceans or other larvae.

Many adult marine organisms produce countless thousands of larvae because their chances of survival are so slim. Besides predation there are also dangers from pollution or other changes in water chemistry and if no suitable food is available they may starve.

Yet in spite of all these problems there are aquarists who do breed marine organisms. In the USA Martin Moe has successfully reared thousands of tropical marine fish (see Further Reading). He recommends removing newly hatched larvae to an isolated aquarium, away from predators. This is best done by attracting them towards a bright light in an otherwise darkened tank and then using a siphon to transfer the tiny organisms to their new tank. It is important that the water in the new tank is the same as that from which they were hatched. The water conditions of the rearing tank must be carefully monitored and he recommends frequent partial water changes for, obviously, conventional filtration systems may damage the larvae. The water is best just gently aerated with a pump and airstone. Food is an important factor and there are two major types. The first is for those living near the sea when, by daily introducing natural seawater into the tank, planktonic organisms will be introduced upon which the larvae will feed, though there is of course a danger that a planktonic predator may also be introduced. Introducing natural seawater daily will also have the double purpose of serving in the frequently needed water changes. The second method of feeding newly hatched larvae is by culturing marine organisms called rotifers. These rotifers themselves require special growths of cultured algae on which to feed, so a complicated system must be organized if natural seawater is not available. One possible alternative is to try to culture rotifers using a yeast suspension, or even to offer frozen plankton if it is available. Once the larvae reach a size when they will take newly hatched brine shrimp there is a good chance some will reach adulthood, for soon after this the more conventional and convenient foods will be accepted.

So there is much organization that needs to be done if it looks as if a pair of fish are going to produce eggs. With invertebrates, whose larvae are usually smaller and often metamorphose to change their body form completely whilst in the plankton, it is even more uncertain that they will be reared successfully. But this does not mean no organisms will breed in the aquarium, because some species reproduce in ways that eliminates the pelagic stage which greatly increases the chances of their offspring surviving, so production of young from these species in the aquarium is more likely.

For example, some anemones, such as the beadlet *Actinia*, can breed by parthenogenesis, when the adult produces a mass of young from its mouth. Some marine molluscs, certain whelks for example, lay eggs from which tiny adults emerge and certain echinoderms such as the cushion star also produce tiny adults, eliminating the planktonic phase. Colonial animals established in the aquarium such as sponges, bryozoa or certain Cnidarians will reproduce asexually as the colony gradually increases in size.

There are also certain marine fish which have also dispersed with the planktonic larval stage. In pipefish or seahorses the female lays the eggs in a pouch on the males' underside. There they develop and tiny adults are released. Other fish such as *Zoarces* are viviparous, meaning the female produces living young. Species such as these may therefore reproduce in the aquarium.

So the breeding of marine organisms is possible but it does require specialized extra equipment, time, trouble and most important of all, knowledge and experience. However, this should not stop any one attempting to breed some organisms for it is extremely rewarding to see young creatures produced in the aquarium.

## CONCLUSION

A marine aquarium is much more than one or two fish plus some other strange and novel creatures. Life originated in the sea and of the many organisms that evolved few managed to colonize freshwater or land. Many sea creatures, especially the invertebrates, are totally unfamiliar to most people, but the tank must be more than just novelty value.

It is a marine microcosm in your home providing a view of species that have remained unchanged for millions of years. The successful marine aquarium system will have a balance, and in its maintenance it is important to try to develop an overall and empirical view.

By all means experiment and try to improve the conditions of the aquarium inhabitants, within reasonable limits, but remember by taking animals and plants away from their usual habitat you are undertaking a responsibility to do everything possible to properly maintain them.

Do not take risks or cut corners, and regard everything in the tank as a valuable living treasure, far from its natural habitat. In a properly maintained aquarium you will have a view of fascinating, unusual and beautiful creatures that will be an education and a delight.

# Appendix I Suitable and Unsuitable Organisms for the Aquarium

The text has indicated the suitability of various species and groups for the aquarium, but it might be worthwhile to point out some organisms that are particularly good for a first marine aquarium. Please remember the warnings on overcrowding given in the book.

| | |
|---|---|
| Sea anemones | Most species |
| Polychaete worms | Both errant and sedentary types |
| Chitons | |
| Limpets | Small individuals only |
| Topshells | |
| Whelks | Scavenging varieties, especially *Nassarius* |
| Mussels | |
| Prawns | |
| Squat lobsters | |
| Porcelain crabs | |
| Hermit crabs | |
| Spider crabs | |
| Starfish | |
| Brittlestars | |
| Sea-urchins | |
| Sea-cucumbers | |
| Ascideans | Especially the individual, not the colonial species |
| Fish | Small gobies or blennies are especially suitable (maximum of two) |

There are also some organisms that are best left alone, for a variety of reasons, explained more fully in the text.

Brown algae
Sponges                 Especially large colonies
Jellyfish
Soft corals
Sea-slugs
Scallops
Cephalopods             Octopus, squid, etc.
Certain crabs           The active pugnacious varieties

# Appendix II Conversion Tables

## VOLUME
1 cubic foot = 6.2 UK gallons = 7.5 US gallons
1 UK (imperial) gallon = 1.2 US gallons = 4.5 litres
1 US gallon = 0.8 UK gallon = 3.785 litres
8 pints = 1 gallon (US and UK)

1 cubic foot of seawater weighs about 64 pounds (lbs) or 29 kgs
1 UK gallon of seawater weighs about 10 lbs or 4.536 kgs
1 US gallon of seawater weighs about 8.5 lbs or 3.86 kgs

## WEIGHT

| pounds (lbs) | kilogrammes (kgs) |
|---|---|
| 1 | 0.454 |
| 2 | 0.907 |
| 5 | 2.268 |
| 10 | 4.536 |

## TEMPERATURE

| Centigrade | 0 | 2 | 4 | 6 | 8 | 10 | 12 | 14 | 16 | 18 | 20 | 25 | 30 | 100 |
|---|---|---|---|---|---|---|---|---|---|---|---|---|---|---|
| Fahrenheit | 32 | 36 | 39 | 43 | 46 | 50 | 54 | 57 | 61 | 64 | 68 | 77 | 86 | 212 |

To convert °F to °C $\frac{(°F - 32)}{1.8} = °C$

To convert °C to °F $(°C \times 1.8) + 32 = °F$
or $°F \eqsim (°C \times 2) + 30$

## LENGTH
1 inch (1″) = 2.54 cm
1 foot (1′) = 12 inches = 30.48 cm

## SPECIFIC GRAVITY

| °C | 27 | 24 | 21 | 19 | 14 | 10 |
|---|---|---|---|---|---|---|
| °F | 81 | 75 | 70 | 66 | 57 | 50 |
| SG | 1.022 | 1.023 | 1.024 | 1.024 | 1.025 | 1.026 |

# Further Reading

Moe, Martin, *Marine Aquarium Handbook*, Norns Publishing Co., Marathon, Florida, 1982.

Spotte, Stephen, *Seawater Aquariums*, John Wiley & Sons, London, 1979.

Thompson, T.E. and Brown, G.H., *British Opisthobranch Molluscs*, Academic Press, London, 1976.

# Index

Page numbers indicated in **bold** type refer to illustrations